FINDING OURSELVES in GOD'S STORY

I0806001

"Michele Hershberger is a conversation partner every teen could benefit from having. She is honest, authentic, and non-defensive in addressing real questions, leaving room for uncertainty while remaining anchored in a deep and personal faith. *Finding Ourselves in God's Story* takes Scripture seriously in all its complexity while highlighting the way the sacred story moves, start to finish, relentlessly toward Jesus Christ."

—**MEGHAN LARISSA GOOD**, author of *Divine Gravity: Sparking a Movement to Recover a Better Christian Story* and *The Bible Unwrapped: Making Sense of Scripture Today*

"Michele Hershberger continues to be a voice of truth and faithfulness for Anabaptist faith formation. Her book invites us to know the real Jesus, to have a real faith, and to live that faith out in the world. This book is a great guide for those exploring faith and making a commitment to following Jesus."

—**DANILO SANCHEZ**, pastor and leadership minister for intercultural transformation, Mosaic Mennonite Conference

"I would eagerly and gladly give this book to each young teen to mature adult who wants to make sense of all of God's story and how they can find their place in it. Michele Hershberger has clearly presented the fullness of God's story in such a beautiful way that is gentle and simple enough for those whose journey has just begun. *Finding Ourselves in God's Story* is a resource that will be useful in every church and every home."

—**NATALIE FRISK**, director of curriculum for RaiseUp Faith and author of *Raising Disciples: How to Make Faith Matter for Our Kids*

"With winsome authority and pastoral warmth, Michele Hershberger invites readers to trace the biblical arc of salvation history and find our identity there as disciples of Jesus Christ. Though written with youth in mind, *Finding Ourselves in God's Story* has substance to enrich the faith journey of any reader. The sidebars throughout the book provide background and dialogue that make complex ideas accessible, deal with hard questions, and point to ways that biblical teaching is relevant for today. Thoroughly Anabaptist without disparaging other faith traditions, this up-to-date guidebook will illuminate the Way for any God-seeker young or old."

—**J. NELSON KRAYBILL**, president of Mennonite World Conference (2015–2022) and president emeritus of Anabaptist Mennonite Biblical Seminary

"*Finding Ourselves in God's Story* is a powerful guide for those exploring the Mennonite-Anabaptist tradition, especially for those who didn't grow up in it. As someone who has found my way into the Anabaptist-Mennonite world, this book has been incredibly helpful in understanding its faith, values, and call to discipleship. It offers a thoughtful and engaging perspective on how our personal stories connect with God's larger story of peace, justice, and community."
—**HENDY MATAHELEMUAL**, associate minister for community engagement, Mosaic Mennonite Conference

"Michele Hershberger has helped shape the lives and faith of many young people, and through this book is striving to give others the tools to do the same. She writes about complex theology in a conversational tone and addresses hard questions in ways that honor those wrestling with faith and invite more conversation."
—**MORIAH HURST**, pastor of child, youth, and adult faith formation at Assembly Mennonite Church

"Michele Hershberger knows that the oldest and most compelling form of Christian witness is to tell a story—to tell the story of God's love of the world through Jesus Christ, as known through Spirit and Scripture. She also knows that every generation has to tell the story afresh for its context. *Finding Ourselves in God's Story* offers a clear invitation to Anabaptist youth to make this story their own, with all their passions and doubts, and all their interests in science, sexuality, technology, ecology, and much else. This book is strongly recommended for group study and would make an excellent resource for pre-baptismal instruction. May it contribute to renewal in our church, and above all to a renewed embrace of God's story."
—**JAMIE PITTS**, professor of Anabaptist studies at Anabaptist Mennonite Biblical Seminary, director of the Institute of Mennonite Studies, and editor of *Anabaptist Witness*

"Youth ministry resources become dated very quickly in our fast-paced modern age. How exciting and refreshing to have a follow-up to *God's Story, Our Story*, which I have used for years to prepare youth for baptism. *Finding Ourselves in God's Story* is both succinct and easy to read. It faithfully clings to the biblical story while not shying away from the challenging and inquisitive questions that are on the hearts and minds of today's youth."
—**CALEY ORTMAN**, chaplain and youth pastor at First Mennonite Church of Reedley, California

FINDING OURSELVES in GOD'S STORY

EXPLORING CHRISTIAN FAITH & LIFE

MICHELE HERSHBERGER

FOREWORD BY DAVE M. CSINOS

HERALD PRESS
Harrisonburg, Virginia

Herald Press
PO Box 866, Harrisonburg, Virginia 22803
www.HeraldPress.com

Library of Congress Cataloging-in-Publication Data applied for.

Study guides are available for many Herald Press titles at www.HeraldPress.com.

FINDING OURSELVES IN GOD'S STORY

Harrisonburg, Virginia 22803. 800-245-7894.

Library of Congress Control Number: 2025001646
International Standard Book Number: 978-1-5138-1510-7 (paperback);
978-1-5138-1511-4 (ebook)
Printed in United States of America
Design by Merrill Miller

29 28 27 26 25 10 9 8 7 6 5 4 3 2 1

To my husband, Del Hershberger,

my faithful theological companion on this journey.

I dedicate this book to him in gratitude for his sharp thinking,

his loving support, and his deep passion for the Mennonite church.

Contents

Foreword

THERE ARE MANY METAPHORS that help me make sense of my eclectic spiritual journey. I'm a bit of a denominational mutt, a far-from-purebred specimen with bits of my religious DNA stemming from many breeds of Christianity. Or maybe I'm more of a vagabond who wanders from place to place, offering whatever services and labor I can along the way, but never really calling any one location home. I might also be a sort of groupie who follows Jesus all over the denominational landscape in hopes of getting to know him better.

While my wanderings through Christianity resulted in my pitching my tent among a small Canadian association of progressive, ecumenically-minded Baptists, my faith journey began in the Roman Catholic Church, a rich, vibrant, and ancient branch of the Christian family tree. This means that I was baptized when I was only a few months old, and then I publicly committed to my faith when I was a youth through a celebration of confirmation that in many ways parallels the practice of believers baptism.

I had many recollections of my confirmation while I was reading *Finding Ourselves in God's Story*. It's the kind of book I wish I had when I was preparing for this rite. Yes, the teachers at the Catholic school I attended used interesting textbooks and engaging curriculum to help us go deeper in our faith as we looked toward our confirmation. And my sponsor, a faithful Catholic friend a few years my senior, encouraged me every step of the way, joining me for confirmation classes and suggesting passages of Scripture upon which I should reflect.

The problem was that, while I took steps to grow in my personal faith and I valued the Scriptures and traditions of Christianity, the two—my faith story and the Christian story—didn't seem terribly connected to one another. What did a burning bush, a mountain sermon, or some letters written two thousand years ago have to do with me? I knew that they had meaning for my life. But it could be difficult to reflect on and articulate this meaning as a young adolescent at the dawn of the new millennium.

Michele Hershberger has written a book that is at once insightful, interesting, and impactful. Her gentle invitation to take a trip through God's story and reflect on its meaning for our lives today is a gift to those who are getting ready to publicly profess their faith and move further into the great big family of God. Like a good confirmation sponsor, she patiently accompanies us as we prepare to be sprinkled with the waters of God's love, poured over with the power of the Holy Spirit, and immersed into the way of life to which Jesus calls us, offering wisdom and asking questions to help us make God's story our own.

Let me offer a few pieces of advice as you start your journey into God's story, into your story. First, go slowly. You are embarking on a well-trodden path full of twists and turns. Open yourself to the unexpected, pause and drink in beauty when it finds you, and stop to capture memories along the way. Second, don't go alone. Read this book with family members, friends, or mentors. There will be much to consider as you move through these chapters, and having some fellow travelers to talk with will be a great help. Third, go prayerfully. The story of God is not a Victorian novel for us to analyze or a bestselling series meant to entertain. It is a living, breathing story of God's ongoing relationship with humanity, a tale older than time that has echoed again and again. It is a story that reverberates in our hearts and souls today. So pray your way through this book, knowing that the God whom you will read about on each and every page is the very same God who is weaving your life into this story.

—David M. Csinos, associate professor of practical theology at Atlantic School of Theology

Introduction

Dear Friends Considering Baptism,

You are contemplating a new relationship, a relationship with the God of the Bible. You hope to find yourself in God's Story, as the title of this book implies. But in this complex world, you may wonder what being part of God's Story means. What does it mean to say yes to a relationship with Jesus? What does it mean to consider getting baptized? What difference will it make in your life and in the world?

Most if not all of us want to make a difference in the world. We want to know our purpose, to find deep meaning to our lives, meaning that brings us joy. And we sense that the values and priorities of the dominant culture in North America fall short of fulfilling this longing. We may wonder why, given all our material wealth, many people are not happy. For example, we hear of famous people struggling with addictions. According to some studies, celebrities are more likely to struggle with addictions or commit suicide than the average American. Researchers have a variety of views on this phenomenon, such as the theory that one is more likely to try to become famous to compensate for a traumatic childhood, but the question remains. Why would the people who seemingly have it all—sports stars, Hollywood entertainers, and successful musicians—struggle as much as they do?[1]

Something's missing from the values of the dominant culture. We've been told to look out for number one, and yet that doesn't seem to bring us joy in the long run. Deep down we know there's got to be something more—or at least different. But what is it? What will bring us true joy?

Following Jesus is the best way to experience true joy. And making this commitment public, through baptism, increases that joy. But it's an upside-down kind of joy. You don't suddenly become trouble free, but you don't worry as much as you used to. And you feel a strength rising, an urge to be different. You feel Jesus nudging you to love people that before you may have ignored or brushed off. But it's more than just having better ethics, because you know people of other faiths or who claim no faith at all who are kind and loving. Something has changed as you follow Jesus. You find it easier to love yourself even though you aren't the most popular. You do have a strange joy, even on the tough days.

And yet there are still rough days. You may at times feel like a fish out of water. Sometimes following Jesus is hard. Boring. Sometimes it won't feel like the way to true joy. That's part of the mystery of the Story. This book is calling you into a narrative thousands of years old that explains this upside-down truth, in a way that doesn't answer all your questions, but invites you into the mystery. To understand this truth and have this joy, you have to take a risk and join this Story. You have to trust God enough to take that first step. It's about asking the big questions of life. It's about seeing everything through a new lens.

And what do we mean by the Story? It's the grand narrative of the Bible, the one big Story of God healing the world. While there are other overall themes in the Bible, this book features one: human sin and what God did and is still doing to free us from sin.

It's about relationship, specifically a relationship with Jesus, a relationship that you figure out in community with other followers.

You may ask, is it necessary to have this relationship with Jesus? Can't a person do good deeds and feel joy from being a good person? There is joy inherent in doing good things for others. And I want to be sensitive to the experiences of those who do good deeds without having faith. Over the long haul, though, we need Jesus. We need Jesus because we need healing from the bad things that have happened in our lives. We also need supernatural help to be freed from doing harm to ourselves, others, and creation and to keep us from turning away from God's love. We can't heal ourselves. Only God can.

We need Jesus because without him, we start to perform good deeds for the wrong reasons. We do them to impress others or maybe even control them, or we do good deeds thinking we can earn God's love or even prove our own worth. None of these wrong motivations add up to true joy. And they can sometimes bring more harm to others than good.

We need Jesus because we don't have the strength on our own to live into this Story. We're fooling ourselves if we think we do.

There is something more to this life than becoming rich and famous, more than living for yourself and just being a good person. I don't have all the answers, but I believe that this "something more" is God, the God we can know best through Jesus

Christ. I know this because I have encountered God and Jesus through the Story of God as it's written in the Bible. I've also encountered God and Jesus through relationships with my church family, through my personal experiences, and through the whispering of the Holy Spirit in my life. Along with millions of others throughout history, I have said yes to the Story and have accepted it as my own.

And I have found joy.

A story of joy

One of my dearest friends is a woman who lives in a big city and works at a halfway house for kids in trouble with the law. She doesn't make much money—hardly any—and the kids often get on her nerves. Her duties range from talking to senators about criminal justice to mopping floors. And she beams. She gets tired sometimes and downright worried about her finances, but even when she has mopped one too many floors—she beams. She radiates joy. Why? She knows Jesus loves her more than she'll ever know. She knows that Jesus is taking her difficult work—even mopping floors—and using it to heal others. Sometimes she can see the miracles unfolding. And sometimes she just feels them in her heart.

How this book came to be

At the Mennonite Convention in 2023, in Kansas City, Missouri, I sat down with fifty to seventy-five youth and adults for four hours as we talked. I shared what I considered to be the main stories of the Bible, an abridged version of the same story you're about to read, and they asked me questions. They gave comments. They poured out their hearts. And these marvelous conversations culminated in the sidebars you are about to read. It was an incredible experience because it proved that if we care enough about God and faith to ask the tough questions of life, then God is right there with us. We trust that God honors our questions and that we can better understand these challenging questions as we work at them together. Those four intense hours proved that this faith of ours matters, and we can insist on it being authentic.

The purpose of this book is to help you find yourself in God's Story. I believe this Story can help you find your identity, and not only that, but also find the One who loves you most—God. It gets even better. As we find ourselves in God's Story, we also find our calling, a calling to help others find themselves in God's Story too.

A word for adults reading this book

This book is similar to my earlier catechism book, *God's Story, Our Story*. However, in many ways, it's a new book. Mennonite church leaders from a variety of places called for a new book in large part because a lot has changed.

The world has changed. For better or worse, we live in a postmodern world. This means that people question everything. At first this might seem terrifying to an organization like the church that believes it has timeless values. But it's good news because we should be questioning some of our beliefs and practices. If they are truly from God, they'll stand up to the test. The gift of the postmodern world is our realization that while there is Truth, we are humble enough to say that we can't see that Truth completely. That Truth, for Mennonites, is Jesus. And the questioning doesn't just happen to beliefs outside of Christianity; we question ourselves and our traditions too. With the help of the Spirit, that can be a good thing.

We also live in a world where Christian nationalism is confused with Christianity, a greater problem in the United States than in Canada. *Christianity Today* defines Christian nationalism as "the belief that the American nation is defined by Christianity, and that the government should take active steps to keep it that way. Popularly, Christian nationalists assert that America is and must remain a 'Christian nation'—not merely as an observation about American history, but as a prescriptive program for what America must continue to be in the future." We are tempted to believe that God loves the United States more than other countries and that Christianity should have favored status over other religions that exist in the United States.[2] There are several problems with Christian nationalism. People who subscribe to this ideology often become Christian in name only, and they garner support for unjust political policies by putting Jesus' name on them. Jesus didn't attempt to bring God's kingdom through the Roman Empire, and we must avoid this temptation too.

And our youth have changed. Since the second edition of *God's Story, Our Story* came out eleven years ago, a lot has happened. Youth have access to the world through social media in ways not present even a decade ago. They have a keen awareness that our earth can only handle so much more pollution, mineral extraction, and ozone depletion before our world economies collapse. The COVID-19 pandemic rocked everyone's world, but teens in particular suffered negatively with changes in education and social activities.

The warning signs that researchers such as Christian Smith and Melinda Lundquist Denton gave us have amplified. In their groundbreaking book, *Soul Searching*, Smith and Denton reported that North American youth worship only a Christian-ish God, one who is "moralistic, therapeutic, and deistic."[3] As biblical illiteracy grows, so does this problem. It's interesting that one of the authors' solutions to the problem is that we drench ourselves in *all* the stories of the Bible, and not just in the stories we like or find easy to understand. We are not to skip the stories that are confusing or flinch at the mysteries that won't go away. God is more than a personal attendant we can call on when we get into trouble, more than a God who wants us to share and be polite. We must dive into the biblical story enough to encounter the real God.

Abandonment has also increased, according to the research of Chap Clark, in *Hurt: Inside the World of Today's Teenagers*.[4] More youth than ever feel abandoned by the adults in their lives. Feelings of abandonment can come in the form of adults rejecting youth, expecting too much from them, or simply not being there when youth need them. Many teens are hurting. At the 2011 Mennonite Church USA youth convention, more than three thousand youth and adults wrote about their pain on small pieces of paper and turned them in as records of the pain of addictions, broken relationships, shame, and fear. We prayed over their words and wondered why there was so much pain.

And the church has changed. Since the first edition of *God's Story, Our Story*, Mennonite Church USA and Mennonite Church Canada have shrunk in size. Denominational loyalty is waning. The polarization gripping our secular societies has made its way into our churches as well. Some of these trends can be linked to the end of Christendom. Christendom is a catchphrase that combines several beliefs that are, to use the term from above, Christian-ish. For example, Christendom assumes that most if not everyone in the society is Christian, primarily because they are citizens of the state. It's culturally appropriate to say you're a Christian even if you don't really know who Jesus is. Paradoxically, being a Christian can be synonymous with being nice in a generalized way or the opposite—being a judgmental person who sees herself as a culture warrior. Christendom functioned positively in our own denominations as an incentive for people to show up at the church building on Sunday mornings. Cultural pressure helped to boost attendance. But it has had a much more damaging effect because we forgot that becoming a Christian is a choice, not just a set of activities good people do. So, perhaps what feels like a bad thing—the end of Christendom—is a gift.

The "why" of this book

This book seeks to dance the delicate dance of holding the authentic questions of our youth together with our need for a common understanding of what it means to follow Jesus. Our youth need the Story to help them find their way to Jesus and true joy. Our youth need truth.

First, we need a *specific truth*. In a culture that says "I'm okay, you're okay, and we can all believe whatever we want," we need something to hang our hats on. I don't believe that all religious beliefs have equal value, or even that all Christian beliefs have equal value. If I did, I'd choose to be a different kind of Christian. While it's good to question things, all of us need a Story that can help provide the context for those questions. Our youth need differentiation; that is, they—and we—need a core set of beliefs and values, even if at times we need to push against what is established. We need a starting point. We need a common faith language.

Second, we need *contextualized truth*. Too many times in the past, adults have tried to teach Christian values and beliefs in a series of propositional truth statements. These statements made sense to us because we had a good sense of the overall biblical narrative in our back pockets. But that's not true for our youth anymore. And even if it were true, our teens want to know how these truth statements came to be and how they fit together. Our youth need to know why God said this or that, and the Story helps provide those answers. The other gift of truth within a grand narrative is that it helps us grasp that truth's complexity. God's best way of communicating with us was by becoming a baby in first-century Palestine and living among us. Talk about contextualization! But many times, Jesus can only be understood as we ponder his context. We must ask ourselves what the original audience thought when they experienced his kindnesses and his miracles, what they learned as they heard his mysterious parables. It's only when we know the meaning they took from the Jesus they experienced that we can find out what we are supposed to understand and experience ourselves. Truth is more complex than a dot on the wall—a truth statement outside its context.

Most of all, we need *relational truth*. Knowledge by itself cannot transform us. It just can't. Words written on a page can help, but they're not enough. We need something—Someone—beyond us. We need Jesus. And we need not just to know facts about him, but to know him. We desperately need more of us to insist on the real thing—an authentic relationship with the One who created us. This authenticity needs a safe environment to thrive as we aim for nothing short of real. That means real questions, real "I don't know"s, real vulnerability, and real courage to say, "This is what I believe."

So, how do we get there?

Start with humility and openness. We need to realize and admit that even in our best efforts, we can't know truth completely. There will be some mysteries surrounding the Bible and Jesus that we'll never figure out this side of heaven. Frankly, if we think we do have it all figured out, we're in spiritual trouble. Like the religious leaders of John 9, we will be so sure of ourselves that we won't be able to see Jesus when he's standing right in front of us. Our certainty will be our god instead of God. And this is a danger whether we consider ourselves theologically progressive, conservative, or right down the middle. Our humility will help us be open-minded, and the Spirit can only really teach those of us who are open-minded.

This doesn't mean that there is no Truth with a capital *T*. It just means that we as fragile, sinful humans can't see that truth completely. And for Anabaptist Christians, that truth isn't any one teaching, but rather a person—Jesus. Jesus is still alive, still healing people, still speaking to us in whispers and shouts—still showing us truth. Truth truly is more complex than a dot on the wall.

One great Mennonite value is the importance of listening to the local community when discerning truth. We believe that every single person is made in the image of God, and every baptized believer is a member of the priesthood of all believers. Therefore, everyone has an understanding or experience of God that all the rest of us need. Likewise, we believe that none of us is smart enough to see the whole picture to discern truth completely. So, we listen respectfully to each other, with special respect shown to the ones with whom we disagree. It's not that we don't understand the importance of taking an individual stand. That's what believers baptism underscores! We believe that each person, on their own, must choose whether to follow Jesus. No one else can make that decision for an individual. Yet we discern truth together, as a community.

The gift of understanding truth in community is woven into this book. It's the reason why you'll find conversations in the margins. These conversations are based on real conversations I've had with youth and young adults. Some of them happened at the Mennonite Convention in 2023, and some of them happened in Kansas, where I live. The conversations are meant to encourage you to have your own conversations. They communicate the truth that it's okay to not have all the answers, that sometimes you find the answers in other people. That's how God has wired us—for relationship.

Live into the paradox. This book seeks to model what it's like to be a Christian. And being a Christian means being sure of some things—particularly things like knowing Jesus is Lord—and not knowing some things (for example, exactly how God will use you in the future). On the one hand, a catechism should provide its readers specific teachings—in our case, good Anabaptist theology—and a clear call to follow a certain path—in our case, Jesus. I have tried to do this. I'm not shy about highlighting Anabaptist theology because that's the tradition I'm primarily writing from and for. I think Anabaptist theology has much to offer and much to learn from the rest of the ecumenical church.

On the other hand, I'm smart enough to know that I can't know all the truth. My experience is too limited. We need to work together, as a community devoted to following Jesus, to discern how best to follow him.

This value of community is demonstrated by the Trinity. God—Father, Son, and Holy Spirit—dwells in community. This value is also demonstrated by the Bible's high view of the church. Instead of sending us an instructional manual (something that most of the Bible is not), God worked through a people, giving them the free choice to follow or to disobey, and in the midst of this messy story, still God made a way for us to find God and God's love.

Don't forget to obey. Another safeguard Anabaptist Christians emphasize is the idea of obedience as a key to understanding. John 7:17 says, "Anyone who resolves to do the will of God will know whether the teaching is from God or whether I am speaking on my own." What would happen if we paid more attention to the things Jesus says to do that are easy to understand, like taking care of the poor, instead of worrying or spending all our time with the issues that trip us up in their complexity? Would this simple obedience open us up to new understanding? It might be worth it to find out!

Adults, share your stories freely. One of the greatest gifts you can give youth today is your story. In a world of virtual reality, a world where so many things are not as they appear, our youth long for authenticity. When you share your faith journey and include the difficult times as well as the great times, younger people see you as real. And that is a gift of great love.

Understand the medium is the message. God became flesh and became incarnated in the person of Jesus. Through Jesus, we can know God. Sometimes Jesus said things that were hard to understand, but we have the Holy Spirit to guide us into all truth. And so we discern best when we call for the Spirit's help in the midst of community, as Pentecost and the Jerusalem Conference so beautifully illustrate. This book operates within this paradox: saying specific truths *and* inviting conversation.

The church needs both. We need the Truth that isn't a set of teachings, but the living, breathing God, incarnate in Jesus and living in us as the Spirit. That Truth is relational, so sometimes it gets messy. And we need these conversations because they encourage us to listen to each other, knowing that none of us alone can completely comprehend God. The conversations in the margins of this book tell us it's okay to not know everything, okay to disagree as long as we're listening to each other. These messy, authentic conversations written here, and the future ones that will happen as you read this book with others, will open you up to a deeper understanding of the Truth that is Jesus.

Let the conversations begin.

Anabaptism, believers baptism, and Mennonites

Anabaptism is an umbrella term for several Christian denominations that emphasize believers baptism and a separation of church and state. The Anabaptist movement began in 1525 when a small handful of people rebaptized themselves in defiance to the government. These original Anabaptists ("rebaptizers") had been baptized as babies to become members of the official state church. They rebaptized each other because they longed for a church free from government control; they didn't want their faith to be used as a tool to promote what the government wanted to do, including things like war, overtaxation, and other unjust things. Finally, they interpreted the Bible to say that one's primary loyalty was to God, not any government.

Today, people in the Anabaptist tradition usually are not baptized as babies. They get baptized after they have made a commitment to follow Jesus and have taken instruction from the church in preparation for that commitment. We call this believers baptism. We call the instruction catechesis and use a specific book called a catechism.

Mennonite Christians are part of this larger group of Anabaptists. They have some differences with other Anabaptists but also many commonalities. Mennonites took their name from an early Anabaptist leader, Menno Simons.

Confession of Faith in a Mennonite Perspective outlines the shared beliefs of Mennonite Church USA and Mennonite Church Canada. Find the summary of this document on page 183.

TOPICS IN CHAPTER 1

- God sets the stage—a good creation
- People in God's image
- God—far off and up close
- Humanity's problem—sin
- God's judgment and God's grace

STORYLINE

- Creation
- Adam and Eve
- Tower of Babel

1. Beginnings

Voice A: What do you say to people who think it's clear that God created the earth in six twenty-four-hour days and then rested on the seventh day? And to others who say creation took millions of years?

Voice B: I've heard that you can take Genesis 1 a lot of different ways, different interpretations that play with time and stuff like that.

Voice A: I believe in the big bang theory, but my family doesn't.

Voice B: Isn't there a verse somewhere along the lines of a day to God is like a thousand years?

Michele: We have to consider genre, or the category of literature. Genesis 1 sounds more like a poem than a science book, with all its beautiful repetition. Poems are just as true as science books; they're just true in a different way. They use symbolic language, which you don't take literally most of the time.

Voice A: So, a "day" could mean a long time?

Michele: Yes. While I believe that God could have created the earth in just six days, or even a nanosecond, contemporary science teaches that the earth is more likely billions of years old, and that doesn't contradict the creation accounts when read in their genre.

THE BIBLE MAKES A BIG DEAL about God as Creator of the world. It opens with the Divine Being calling the world into being and doing it with intention and love (Genesis 1–2). We are blessed with the gift of science to help us understand our incredible universe, and we can embrace this gift without losing God's personal involvement and intention in creation. The Bible tells the creation story differently than other ancient creation stories where the gods create the world by violence. We Christians take by faith that God spoke the word and the world came into being. We believe God made a beautiful, perfect creation and God created it peacefully. Truly, "God saw everything that he had made, and indeed, it was very good" (Genesis 1:31).

Some ancient religions would have called nature divine—part of God—while others saw the physical world as corrupt and not worth saving. But the ancient followers of God understood creation, including human beings, in a third way. Creation is good and has value, but it is not God. On one hand, God called the physical world good. If that's true, then it changes how we must treat our bodies and the rest of nature. We have a responsibility to care for what God has called good. God calls us to be caretakers of the physical world (Genesis 1–2), to tend to the earth like a gardener tends to her garden. Climate change threatens our quality of life, and for some it threatens their very lives. Currently, the oceans are filling up with plastic bottles and the ozone layer is depleted by the fumes of our cars. God calls us to respond, to love the world God created.

Some of us have been told that our bodies are worthless or unredeemable. We hate our freckles, how tall we are (or aren't), or whatever.

But God said creation was good.

Some of us don't associate with people who look different than us or hold different beliefs.

But God said creation was good.

We're all tempted to use pesticides and single-use plastic for convenience.

But God said creation was good.

On the other hand, nature—from mountains to trees to our bodies—is not to be worshiped. Sometimes humanity has been tempted to worship creation instead of the Creator, and that gets us in trouble. That's why we see an emphasis on the sin of idolatry in the Bible (see Exodus 20:4–6; also p. 62)

Humans are made in God's image

Our bodies are good because God created nature and the physical world in an intentional way. But humans are also special because every one of us, in the fullness of humanity, has been created in God's image (Genesis 1:26–27). Like God, we have free will. Like God, we are spiritual beings.

Voice A: What does it mean to be made in the image of God?

Michele: It means we are wonderfully made, even though that may be hard to believe sometimes. And I think it's hard to believe because of all the social media we take in.

Voice B: What does "made in the image of God" mean if you're queer?

Michele: We believe that God made all people in God's image. Equally good and beloved.

Voice A: But, that's not what my church says.

Michele: I'm sorry. This is difficult. I know people on both sides of the conversation who want to do the right thing, people on both sides who want to be loving. I ache that it's so challenging.

Voice B: It's a hard thing to work through because there are Bible verses that say it's wrong. It says that God created them "male and female."

Michele: Yes, I know that verse in Genesis. Genesis 1 also says "night and day," yet there are degrees to consider. What is sunrise? Is it day or night? The text talks about waters and dry land. So, what are the swamps, dry land or the waters?

Voice A: I have queer friends who love Jesus with all their heart.

Michele: It's important to listen to the stories of people who have a different sexual orientation or gender identity than the majority culture. We are called by God to listen to others and be kind, especially when our beliefs differ. Yes, there are Bible verses that don't seem to support same-sex marriage, but Jesus doesn't say anything about the issue directly. The Bible says that those who testify and live out "Jesus is Lord" are his followers. People can do this irrespective of gender identity, sexual orientation, ethnicity, or other intrinsic qualities (things you can't change). I know queer people who truly have Jesus as their Lord. I think we need to keep our hearts and minds open. God created all of us in God's image.

God is far off and up close. The book of Genesis gives us two creation stories that show us two different pictures of God. In Genesis 1, we see God as all-powerful, mighty, and high above us. God speaks the word, and worlds are created. This shows God's transcendence—God is above us, beyond us, too mysterious for us to know, too awesome for us to do anything for but worship. Then in Genesis 2, we see God in another way—God as one who is up close and relational. God walks on the earth and gently bends down to form Adam's body from the earth. These two images complement each other. We need both the high God

Voice A: How do you reconcile two creation stories, side by side?

Michele: I love that you're asking this question. I think they're both needed because I think God is both untouchable and beyond our reach (as shown in the first creation story) *and* close up and personal (as shown in the second creation story). And God is both, all at the same time.

Voice B: Okay, but what do we do with the idea of a flat earth? You can find Bible verses that essentially say the earth is flat, but we know the earth to be round. So, is the Bible really inspired by God or not?

Michele: Another great question. What do you think?

Voice B: God didn't care about setting the record straight. God was working with the culture of the people. Or not everything was inspired by God.

Voice A: I don't really care about whether science can prove that the Bible is true. I think, ultimately, we have to choose to believe. Since there is plenty of evidence that there is a God, people who don't believe in God have to admit they are making a choice not to believe.

Voice B: What if belief is more than just a choice?

Michele: That's something to think about. What is the purpose of the Bible? I think it's to point us to a loving God.

Which aspect of God are you more comfortable with—the up close and personal God or the all-powerful, mysterious God?

Who is God?

Unimaginable.

Unpredictable. Think about all those times in Scripture where God is described as angry.

Yeah, but is that really what God was feeling? Or just how it felt to the people at that time? What is God like? Look at Jesus.

and the personal God (Isaiah 6:1–11). One image of God, one creation story, can't communicate all there is to know about God's character. God is both close up and personal *and* far off and beyond knowing.

God is a mystery . . . yet we know God through Jesus. The two creation stories present the first paradox about God, who is far off and unknowable yet close up and personal. Jesus continued the paradox. Christians believe he was completely God, including all the wonderful things about God we can't begin to comprehend. And all that awesomeness became a human baby. We understand Jesus as God in the flesh, arriving on the scene much later than the beginning of the universe, so to mention Jesus at creation might seem odd. But the gospel of John says that the world was created through Jesus (John 1:3). In fact, the first chapter of John echoes the Genesis 1 story. John makes the point that Jesus, the

Word, was in the beginning and helped create the world. The creator later "became flesh"—a person just like you and me (John 1:14). What an incredible way to begin to know and understand what is absolutely beyond our understanding! Jesus walked on the earth, feeling pain and hunger, struggling with the temptation to sin, laughing at jokes until his sides split. The unknowable became knowable through Jesus. What a gift to us!

Christians talk about God being omnipresent (everywhere), omniscient (knowing everything), and omnipotent (all powerful). Yet those terms alone don't fully describe God. In Jesus, the all-powerful One came to earth and showed us who God really is by walking with people, loving them, and allowing himself to be rejected, cursed, beaten, and eventually crucified. That combination of omnipotence and obedient love, even to the point of death, is found in no one other than Jesus. This is the beautiful, unique love of Jesus.

We know God through creation, through word pictures, through stories in both the Old and New Testaments and through Jesus. The beauty of nature testifies to God's power and creativity. The Bible is also creative, using dozens of metaphors to tell us characteristics of God. God is like a warrior (Psalm 3). God is pictured as a shepherd in Psalm 23, and Jesus reintroduces that metaphor and applies it to himself in John 10, along with the metaphor of a mother hen in Luke 13:34. We also know God through individual stories in the Bible. We see God's omniscience at work as the prophets tell the kings that God saw their evil deeds. We see God's omnipotence in mighty miracles, and we observe God's omnipresence as God walks with the Israelites through the wilderness.

paradox:
a seemingly contradictory statement that expresses a possible truth

The Bible uses *paradoxes* to describe God because God cannot be limited to any straightforward description.

What does it mean to have a relationship with God? How is it more than just saying yes to a set of statements about God?

Most of all, we know God through Jesus. We can learn much from the Old Testament but Jesus provides the clearest picture of God (Hebrews 1:1–3; John 1:18).

What is God like?

The Bible uses dozens of metaphors—word images—to tell us what God is like. Three of them, among many, are

- God as a mother eagle (Deuteronomy 32:11–13)
- God as a warrior (Psalm 3)
- God as a shepherd (Psalm 23; 80:1)

But God can't be summed up by any of these metaphors. Every time we use a metaphor for God, we risk putting God in a box (see Isaiah 40:18–31; Romans 11:33–36). In Genesis 3:8, for example, God is portrayed as walking through the Garden of Eden. Do we understand God literally to have feet, or is the writer using such language to help us grasp something that is beyond explanation?

God wants a relationship with humans. One seventeenth-century summary of Christian faith from the Reformed tradition, the Westminster Longer Catechism, states that our purpose in life is to "glorify God and to enjoy him forever." From the Bible's opening pages, it is clear that God also wants to enjoy *us*! We can see God's longing for relationship in the creation stories. God walked in the garden, talking with Adam and Eve. And God gave them choice, whether or not to refrain from eating the forbidden fruit of the tree of knowledge and the tree of life (Genesis 2–3). Even after they sinned, God sought them out, calling their names (Genesis 3:9) and caring for them. In a nutshell, that's what the rest of the Story is about. It's a beautiful tale of the loving Creator seeking out the beloved creation—you and me—to communicate one thing: I love you.

Things fall apart with the problem of sin

One way to read the biblical story is to see sin as the primary problem that God, through God's people and ultimately through Jesus, is working to overcome. According to this reading, humans soon make choices that are wrong and against God's will. And with that choice comes the problem that is at the center of the Story's development: sin. The Bible begins with four stories in close succession that show different perspectives of the human problem of sin. We see four major relationships broken: our relationship with God, our relationship with our inner selves, our relationship with others, and our relationship with the rest of creation. We also see how sin becomes more complicated as it snowballs into increasingly bad situations.

From the first moment, God was not content to let sin ruin these relationships. God begins the beautiful work of creating shalom. *Shalom* is a Hebrew word that we translate as peace. Both words, if understood correctly, mean more than just an absence of war. Shalom means that the four relationships broken by sin start being healed. We are forgiven and reconciled with God. The Spirit helps us love others, even our enemies. We grow in our care for the earth and our bodies, and we work to make sure everyone has enough to eat and drink. God even helps us love ourselves. This is a true picture of God's shalom.

Voice A: Now I'm confused. I thought we were supposed to try to be like God.

Michele: We are called to be godly, but that's different from being our own god and thinking we have control.

Voice B: Wow, even Christians can fall into that trap.

Story 1. Trying to be like God. In the first story, Adam and Eve want to become God. The serpent contradicts God's instructions not to eat the fruit from the tree of the knowledge of good and evil. Eating the fruit, it says, will make them "like God" (Genesis 3:5). Adam and Eve are led to believe that they will become "wise" (3:6). In some ways, sin is trying to be like God. When one person kills another, it can be seen as a form of bringing on judgment that only God can give. When we judge other people, we assume we know best, or at least that we know the whole story.

The Bible's answer to the question, Where does sin come from? is that it comes from both outside pressures and our own distorted desires. Adam and Eve are tempted by the outside influence of the serpent, but they also cave in to their distorted longings. And the effects are devastating. They feel a brokenness in their relationship with God, with each other as they blame each other, and with themselves. Feeling shame for the first time, they cover their

Voice A: I don't really like this story. Everybody gets destroyed?

Voice B: Exactly, and do you expect me to believe that two of every single kind of animal are put on this boat? It'd have to be really big.

Voice A: And this is somehow God's grace?

Michele: This story is a tough one. The importance of this story is to show the depth of sin's effects on individuals and all of creation, and that lesson is more important than whether the flood and the ark happened in a literal sense. (I mean, yes, it'd have to be a big boat.)

Voice B: The part about all of humanity drowning—that's a difficult one.

Michele: I agree. Did the people just not yet understand God completely and so they interpreted the story this way, or did God allow the natural consequences of their actions to play out against them? I don't know. I'm not going to pretend my judgment is better than God's. The actions of God reported here surely don't sound like Jesus. But I encourage you to hang on. There's more to the story.

nakedness. Even the ground is cursed (Genesis 3 :17–19). And as the second story shows, sin affects the family.

Story 2. Pursuing violence out of jealousy. Adam and Eve's son Cain feels jealousy toward his brother Abel. When God accepts Abel's offering, the first of the lambs born to his flock, and rejects Cain's offering of the first of his vegetables, Cain gets angry and jealous. God tells him that he must master his evil desires. But instead, Cain kills Abel, committing the first act of violence. Here we can see how a broken relationship with self—Cain's jealousy and inability to accept critique—leads to broken relationships with others. Abel is dead and Cain is cut off from God and from others as he wanders the earth (Genesis 4:1–16).

Story 3. Taking the whole world down. Soon the whole human population is full of wickedness (Genesis 6–9). So God asks Noah to build a big boat called an ark, for soon God will send a flood that will cover the whole earth. The ark holds Noah's family and two of every kind of animal. With this unusual rescue plan, there is the promise of continued life. In this story, sin not only destroys human relationships, but almost all of creation as well.

Story 4. Alienation and the confusion of language. The snowball of sin continues. Like Noah's ark, the Tower of Babel impacts the whole world (Genesis 11:1–9). Here, the people want to make a name for themselves by building a tower that reaches to the heavens. They believe that climbing to the top of this tower will put them over the dome of the sky, making them gods. Like Adam and Eve, the people want to be God, wise in their own eyes. Their efforts are stalled when God confuses their common language so that, suddenly speaking in different tongues, they can't understand each other. Community is broken, and the people scatter apart from each other.

In all these stories, we see sin breaking relationships between humans and God, among one another, and between themselves and the created world. That's the problem with sin. And it's so slippery because we don't set out to break relationships. We set out—in sometimes very subtle ways—to be God, which is obvious in the first and the last stories. In the middle two stories, where violence is a problem, this violence is perhaps the most extreme way we try to be God, by taking life into our own hands.

The problem of sin affects everything

Sin yields devastating results in our lives. Unfortunately, many people today don't want to talk about it. We may want to talk about how horrible Hitler was, but we don't want to talk about how we bad-mouthed the new kid in school or how we stole someone's AirPods. These sin stories in the Bible paint a clear picture of the relationships ruined by sin and its snowball effect on all of humanity.

Sometimes we are the victim instead of the offender—the sinned against rather than the sinner. Sometimes we're Cain and sometimes we're Abel, and sometimes we're a mixture of both. Sometimes we are tremendously influenced by outside forces, and sometimes it's nobody's fault but our own. There are individual sins, actions that go against God's will, and all of us commit those actions. There's also systemic sin, evil that's bigger than us, a power that impacts entire organizations, a force that hurts humanity. This systemic sin is what the New Testament refers to when it talks about "the powers" or "rulers" (see 1 Corinthians 2:6,

Truth and consequences

1. Sin is hurting people, disobeying God, or hurting yourself.
2. Sin is hurting creation. (I don't pour poison into our streams, but I buy cheap products from corporations that do. Just by driving a car, I participate in a sinful system that hurts the physical world.)
3. Sin is not doing the good thing you were called to do.
4. Sin is bigger than individuals. Sin creeps into our systems. (I benefit from being white. I don't walk around being overtly racist, but I don't do much to stop racism either.)

Ephesians 1:20–21, Colossians 2:15). But whether it's individual or systemic sin, it wreaks havoc.

Part of being made in God's image includes the gift of free will. Every person has choices. God does not force us to do anything. God wants us to make the right choice out of love and gratitude, and in order for that choice to be free, God also had to give us the freedom to choose to sin. So, a tension remains. How can God guarantee that everything will work out in the end and, at the same time, give us the freedom to choose? How can justice win out and God's kingdom come if God refuses to force our obedience and continues to give us the right to mess things up? These are challenging questions to wrestle with.

How is sin controlling your life? What relationships is sin tearing apart? To whom will you go for help?

Because of the great power of sin and its ability to make a giant mess, the choice to obey God is sometimes very difficult. It feels like we really aren't free to choose. Evil affects individuals, creating chaos and heartache for them and their relationships. It is also true that evil, or Sin with a capital *S*, can be a part of whole systems: governments, institutions, organizations, and even something as simple as a group of friends.

If God controls the world, is it more like the mechanical control of a well-oiled machine, or the adaptive guidance of a loving parent? And who's to blame when things seem out of control? Is "control" even the best way to think about how God relates to creation?

Think about your experience at school. There is a negative group dynamic that can happen—pecking orders, who's cool, who's not, people compromising their morals just to get into a group. Those are powers. It's not that having a group is always evil or that any one individual in a group sets out specifically to cause harm. But what starts out as good, or at least neutral, can turn ugly when sin comes into play. There, too, the power of sin can be especially devastating.

grace: *the freely given, unmerited favor and love of God*

The judgment is the grace. How does God respond to this awful power of evil? God responds with grace and love, as a loving parent might do. God works to create shalom. God is not a white-haired, stern figure just waiting with glee to zap us when we sin. True, there are negative consequences when we sin, but these consequences also help bring us back into relationship with God. Cain is a good example. Cain was marked and had to wander the earth as a consequence for his sin. But the mark also offered protection because it meant that no one could kill him. The people building the Tower of Babel were forced to quit their project, which was good since the project was futile and dangerous. In these stories we see a connection between judgment and grace.

Think about getting in trouble at school and receiving detention. It's judgment, but what if that wakes you up to the fact that you need to straighten up?

A central theme in the Story, which we'll examine in the next chapters, is how God works with the problem of sin. Sin ushers in problems and judgment, and it is everywhere. But far greater than the power of sin are God's power and willingness to heal and forgive and to bring us to where we were created to be. The real story is this: God jumps through hoops and bends over backward to show how deeply God loves us and wants to be in relationship with us! We do, however, have to take sin seriously. If we see the problem of sin as something we only commit against God, then we will emphasize only the part of the story that deals with restoring our relationship with God. In that case, our main job would be to decide whether we believe in Jesus. But if the problem of sin is broken relationships not only with God, but also with others, self, and creation, then true salvation addresses and heals all of those relationships.

God understands the implications of this awful sin mess. God has a plan. And that plan is the next part of the Story.

The big conversation

Voice A: You say that God's judgment is also God's grace. What do you do with the "wrath of God?" There's no grace in that.

Voice B: Additionally, it seems there is a difference between how God behaves when it comes to different passages of Scripture about judgment and grace.

Michele: I hear you. The God presented in some parts of Scripture seems different than the God presented in others, and many people interpret the God of the Old Testament as purely wrathful. But on the flip side, maybe we've overlooked some of the verses in the Old Testament that do show grace, such as those that state God has mercy for a thousand generations (Deuteronomy 7:9) and that God doesn't visit the sin of the parents on the children anymore (Ezekiel 18).

Voice B: Anymore? So, God *used* to do that? Ugh. That doesn't seem any better.

Voice A: Give God a break here. Maybe Ezekiel is helping people finally see who God really is. That God has always been more gracious than angry.

Voice C: Yes, but the "wrath of God" happens a lot in the Bible. Isn't God angry about sin?

Michele: I think God loves us, and in that love, God doesn't want sin to hurt us. God loves us better than the best human parent loves their child. Sometimes the loving thing to do is let natural consequences unfold and sometimes the loving thing to do is to set limits to prevent even more severe consequences (think about the times you've been grounded by your parents).

Voice A: Or maybe all those "wrath of God" phrases are people getting it wrong. People may have attributed the natural consequences of sin to God even when they weren't from God. But God let them write those words down anyway, respecting their free will... which would mean that God allowed mistakes in the Bible.

Voice C: Yes, but then you could say that there are mistakes throughout the entire Bible!

Michele: You could. These are complicated concerns! We'll keep talking about how God longs to communicate with us by inspiring the biblical writers to chronicle certain ideas and events. At the same time, God did not force the biblical writers' hands to record specific words. There are several Bible verses indicating the prophets didn't quite get it right (Hebrews 1:1–3). And as Mennonite Christians, we solve this problem of conflict within scripture by looking to Jesus when the Bible seems to say two different things.

Summing it up

- *God is the creator of a good universe.* We take by faith that God created everything. From the Bible, we understand that the created world is good. In particular, people are created in God's image.
- *God is both beyond knowing and knowable.* The Bible presents two accounts of creation not because there were two creations, but because telling the story from two perspectives demonstrates how God is both all-powerful and yet personal and up close.
- *Sin harms our relationship between God and us, as well as our relationships with self, others, and all creation.* Sin is not about hurting God's feelings. When we sin, relationships are hurt. Sin takes many forms and is found everywhere, both in individuals and in whole systems. Sometimes we are the sinners, and at other times we are the ones who are sinned against.
- *Judgment and grace are flip sides of the same coin.* From the beginning of the Bible, we see that God's judgment on sin is not mean-spirited punishment. It is always tied to God's desire to restore right relationships with God, our inner selves, others, and creation.

A spiritual discipline to practice

Write the ABCs along the left-hand side of a piece of paper. Then list one or two names or descriptions of God for each letter. Your list might look like this: A = almighty, awesome, all-powerful; B = beautiful, bountiful, and so on.

TOPICS IN CHAPTER 2

- God chooses people
- God's providence
- Salvation
- From bondage to freedom in the wilderness
- New way of being God's people
- Good rules for living
- Holy war—let God defend you
- Worship
- Shalom

STORYLINE

- Abraham and Sarah
- Moses
- God rescues the Israelites from slavery
- Ten Commandments

2. God Creates Again

IT'S DISCOURAGING TO SEE ALL THE EVIL in the world. At times it feels like nobody cares, that people are bullies, that big corporations are taking advantage of their workers and of our earth. We are left wondering: Does God really have a plan to fix this mess? Where is God in all of the suffering and chaos? In this chapter, we will cover God's presence in the world and God's ongoing response to humanity. The good news is that God does respond, as God did right at the beginning of human history. God creates again. Only this time, God creates a group of people who know and obey God.

God calls Abraham and Sarah and creates a people

Try to imagine this: you are an ordinary man in the Middle East about four thousand years ago. You're sitting by a campfire with your wife, and you hear a voice. You don't see anything, but you sense something—outside of you, but inside of you as well. Is it indigestion? Or is it someone (Someone?) speaking to you? The voice continues. It wants you to drop everything and just start moving to some new place you don't know about. You check the bushes. Nobody there. You pinch yourself. Nope. Not dreaming. You sense that something extraordinary is going on.

That is the story of Abram. In ways we can only imagine, God communicated with this man and his wife, Sarai, telling them to drop everything and start walking to, well, wherever. But why them? The Bible speaks of God choosing Abraham's family for a special mission (Genesis 12). It doesn't mean Abraham and his people were God's favorites to the exclusion of all others. In fact, God tells Abraham and Sarah that in them, "all the families of the earth shall be blessed" (Genesis 12:3). Abraham and his descendants had a choice: Would they obey this Voice?

Voice A: Does God have favorites? You can point to a lot of Bible verses that make it sound like God has a favorite people—specifically, the Jews.

Michele: God does love the Jews, and he chose to bless them so they could be a blessing to all people. I see the whole Bible as a story of inclusion. God chose Abraham in order to choose others. All of us are chosen to choose others. We're chosen for a mission.

So God creates a people, working with four families, beginning with Abraham and Sarah. They had one son, named Isaac. Isaac married Rebekah and they had twins, Esau and Jacob. Jacob deceived his minutes-older twin brother out of the firstborn privileges and became the male head of the third family. He married Leah and Rachel. Jacob wrestled with God and through this encounter was given the name Israel, which means one who wrestles with God and humans and has prevailed (Genesis 32:28). From Jacob's twelve sons, Joseph (the eleventh but the oldest of Jacob's favorite wife, Rachel) became part of the fourth family. He married Asenath, an Egyptian woman.

All four families endured many struggles, and in each family, God intervened and miraculously rescued them. Some Christians call this divine involvement in our lives *providence*. Abraham and Sarah, the first family, had no descendants and were way past the age of childbearing. But God did the miraculous, and despite some lack of faith (Sarah even laughed at God), Isaac was born to them in their old age (see Genesis 12–18, 21). Isaac didn't trust God. He told a lie about his wife, Rebekah, saying she was his sister so he wouldn't get killed. Jacob deceived his father, Isaac, and then had to flee the wrath of Esau. (See Genesis 12:10–20, 16:1–15, 18:1–15, 26:6–11, 27:1–40, 29:15–30.) God rescued this family despite natural limitations like barrenness, and human unfaithfulness and stupidity. These people were not always the best examples of godliness—yet God used them. God wants to partner with humans, especially the ones who respond to God's call, despite our flaws and foibles.

Perhaps the strangest story of providence revolves around Joseph (Abraham and Sarah's great-grandson). Already his father's favorite son, Joseph bragged to his brothers that someday they would bow to him (Genesis 37:1–11). The brothers couldn't take it anymore, and so they threw Joseph in a pit and then sold him into slavery in Egypt. But what seemed to be terrible news for Joseph turned out to be what saved this same family.

Eventually, Joseph rose to power as one of Egypt's top leaders. He stored up enough food for a famine that would sweep the entire Middle East. His brothers—the same ones who sold him into slavery—came down to Egypt from where they lived, Canaan, looking for food. They bowed in reverence before Joseph, not knowing this powerful leader was their own brother. The hated one became the hero when he gave his family food. More importantly, through God's providence, the family was kept alive to keep developing God's Story (see Genesis 37–50 for more details).

Joseph's story not only illustrates God's divine providence, but also shows us that God loves all people and wants to use us as a way to bless all people. Many people emphasize how he saves his family from famine, even the very brothers who sold him into slavery. But he also saves the Egyptians and other neighboring countries. Joseph was chosen to bless non-Israelites. God does love everyone!

providence:
a manifestation of divine care or direction

salvation:
*God's work to bring creation back to what it was meant to be. Included in salvation are at least three strands of good news: God heals the four broken relationships (**see p. 32**), freeing us from the power and consequences of sin; God makes us into new people; and God works in us to bring God's healing and hope to our world.*

Salvation is really at the heart of the story and comes up over and over in this book.

Salvation, part 1: leaving slavery

It would seem like everything is just fine with the people of God. Jacob and his children and grandchildren moved from Canaan to Egypt to escape the widespread famine (Genesis 46). For a while, their story seems on track. The family grows and prospers. But a new pharaoh comes to power who doesn't know about Joseph and his family (Exodus 1:8–14). This pharaoh takes one look at these foreigners who are doing so well and he enslaves them. The slavery was torture and the oppression severe. But the more the Israelites were oppressed, the more they multiplied. So, Pharaoh decrees that every Israelite baby boy should be thrown into the Nile River (Exodus 1:22). Now the family of God is in trouble like never before. It is time for God to show not just providence, but salvation.

The God who had been merciful all along, the God who had showered the Israelites with steadfast love, is the same God who hears their cries for help. God's help comes in the most unlikely form: an Israelite baby floating in a basket in the Nile River. His name is Moses. His mother had hidden him there to escape the fate of the other enslaved male babies. God honors her step of faith. The pharaoh's daughter picks Moses up out of the water, and the baby slated for death becomes the new son of the palace instead.

Although Moses grew up in Pharaoh's palace, he somehow identifies with his own people. One day he sees an Egyptian beating one of his kinsfolk and it is more than he can bear. He kills the Egyptian taskmaster and then flees for his own life into the wilderness (Exodus 2).

Moses hears the Voice. Pharaoh didn't find Moses, but God does. It is there in the desert that Moses sees a bush on fire, yet not consumed (Exodus 3). From the bush comes a voice—the Voice who

Michele: The God of the Bible acts in history. Some of us may be tempted to believe that God is a "sit on the clouds just watching what people are going to do" kind of a God. On the contrary, God is involved, in the middle of the game, actively present. We can see this clearly in the Moses story. God is free to act, and so are we, either for good or bad.

Voice A: So what?

Michele: First, we worship God for a different reason. We worship and give offerings not to get God to do something for us but because God acted first in love. And we don't try to manipulate God into giving us what we want—because it doesn't work.

Voice B: Right—that's not relationship, that's just using God. And if you use God, you'll end up using people too.

Voice A: You mean . . . like oppression?

Michele: Yes. And sometimes God does surprising things that can't be explained. God sometimes gives us what we ask for, even a miracle. And other times God doesn't, and that's so frustrating. It almost makes you not want to believe.

Voice B: But God knows best.

Voice A: Yeah, but that's hard to believe sometimes.

Michele: Yes. The story of God parting the Red Sea for Moses and the Israelites—that's one of those miracle things.

has spoken to his ancestors. "I have observed the misery of my people who are in Egypt," God says. "I know their sufferings, and I have come down to deliver them from the Egyptians. . . . Now go, I am sending you to Pharaoh to bring my people, the Israelites, out of Egypt" (see Exodus 3:7–10). God is going to rescue the Israelites from their slavery with one of the members of Pharaoh's own household!

Moses agrees reluctantly to his assignment and returns to Egypt. Along with his brother Aaron, he asks Pharaoh to let the enslaved people go free. When Pharaoh refuses, God sends ten plagues on Egypt—plagues that miraculously do not hurt those who are enslaved (Exodus 5:1–12:32). The last plague is the deadliest. The angel of death comes to every household, and in every household the firstborn dies. The only ones spared from this terrible fate are the families who put the blood of a lamb on their doorpost (Exodus 12).

I guess if God can use Moses, God can use anyone—even me.

From what kinds of oppression do you need deliverance? Looking back over your life, where has God rescued you?

God's name, YHWH (Yahweh)

At the burning bush, God reveals God's personal name, YHWH (Yahweh), to Moses. Roughly translated, Yahweh means "I AM WHO I AM" or "I will be who I will be" (Exodus 3:13–14), and is translated as LORD in most English Bibles. This name is so special that even today many Jews do not pronounce the name, and many write it without its vowels—YHWH.

In the ancient world, to reveal one's name to another was to initiate a relationship and become vulnerable to that person. That the Creator of the universe would take the initiative to proclaim this personal name to Moses was an unheard-of step toward building relationship between God and humans.

Later Jesus identifies himself as the "I AM." In the book of John, Jesus says, "I am the living bread" (6:51), "I am the true vine" (15:1), "I am the good shepherd" (10:11), and "I am the resurrection and the life" (11:25). His choice of words was no accident; most Jews avoided using the phrase "I AM" out of respect for God. Jesus was calling himself by the same sacred name reserved only for Yahweh.

Pharaoh finally decides to let the enslaved people go free (Exodus 12:33–37). Here the Bible includes an important detail: other people, probably non-Israelites who were also enslaved, join God's people in the exodus (Exodus 12:38). As God told Abraham, God cares not only for the children of Abraham, but for all who suffer under oppression.

Voice B: I never liked this story. Why should someone die for their family's mistakes?

Michele: I don't like it either. We don't always understand and—sometimes—innocent people do suffer for the mistakes of others. I choose, every day, to believe that God is good, that God is love.

Pharaoh, however, changes his mind after sending the Israelites away. It is too convenient to have thousands of enslaved people at his fingertips. He sends an army after the seemingly helpless, unarmed people to bring them back. As they hear the chariots charging after them, the people size up their situation. With Pharaoh's army behind them and the Red Sea in front of them, they know they are trapped. But Moses says, "Do not be afraid, stand firm, and see the deliverance that the LORD will accomplish for you today. . . . The LORD will fight for you, and you have only to keep still" (Exodus 14:13b–14; see p. 51 for a discussion of holy war).

See the Confession of Faith summary of Article 10 about making disciples out of all nations on page 184. God has always wanted an inclusive people of God formed out of all people groups.

God fights and the people stand still. The people hold their breath. Moses said that the Lord would fight for them. But would

Voice A: So, Yahweh does all the fighting at the Red Sea and the Israelites just stand still. But the Egyptian army still gets killed. You said that Abraham and Sarah—and eventually all believers—have been chosen for a mission to bless all the families on earth. How does the Egyptian army get blessed here?

Michele: This is a tough question. I ask the same question about God sending a flood during Noah's time that wiped out the earth's inhabitants. It doesn't feel like they're being blessed. I don't have all the answers, but you can see that throughout all the wars in the Old Testament when people obeyed God and didn't fight, God always performed a miracle for them. The more they trusted Yahweh, the more they were victorious. The prophets pointed to a time when swords will be beaten into plowshares (Isaiah 2:4). Then Jesus came and revealed God's ultimate will, what God really wanted: Jesus taught and lived nonviolence. And they killed him, but God raised him back to life.

God come through? Moses raises up his staff. The pillar of cloud that guided them moves behind them, and a strong east wind blows. Miraculously the waters part. Amazed, the people cross through on dry ground. When the Egyptian army follows them into the sea, the waters go back together and the Egyptian army is drowned. Safe on the other shore, Moses's sister Miriam leads them in a celebration to God (Exodus 15:20).

It was there, on the other side of the Red Sea, that this motley crew of mixed peoples became a people. It was here, having experienced such a dramatic rescue, that they bonded as one—the Israelites. They had experienced the salvation of God. This deliverance from slavery would be the story that would sustain the people of Israel throughout their history. It was at the center of who they were.

How hard is it for you to stand still and let God fight for you like the Israelites did? Should this way of living apply only to our individual lives or should we also trust God when we have national enemies? Check out the Confession of Faith summary for Article 22 on page 185 and discuss what it means.

Salvation is spiritual and physical. Sometimes we like to think of salvation as just an individual, spiritual experience. In the exodus story, salvation means physical freedom from an oppression that is literally killing the people. God does care about the spiritual oppression that we all suffer because of sin. But God also cares about physical injustice and oppression. If salvation brings back together everything that sin breaks apart, then somehow it must mean good news for those who suffer physically as well as those who suffer spiritually.

The exodus story is retold and celebrated often in the Old Testament. At least six of the Psalms (78, 105, 106, 114, 135, 136) remember God's deliverance of the people from Egypt. The prophets often refer to the exodus when they summon the people back to God (Isaiah 11:16; Jeremiah 2:6; 7:22–25; Ezekiel 20:6, 10). Passover is the Jews' annual commemoration of the exodus. At the Passover meal, Jesus explains the "new covenant" through his own body and blood (Luke 22:20; see also pp. 58, 95, 140).

Salvation, part 2: a new way of being

Physical deliverance wasn't the end of the story for the Israelites. They were in great need of deliverance from their sin and messed-up thinking. Ironically, those who were formerly enslaved began complaining about the lack of food almost as soon as they were out of Egypt. They longed to go back to the pots of meat of Egypt (Exodus 16:3). This was a case of mass amnesia, as the newly freed Israelites remembered only the security and not the hardship of the good old days. They needed physical deliverance from death-dealing slavery, and they also needed new hearts. They needed to learn how to be the people of God.

In the wilderness, God not only provides food for them (see Exodus 16:4–35), but also sets out to help them understand a whole new way of living. God begins by issuing the Ten Commandments. At Mount Sinai, the same place where Moses met the burning bush, God speaks to Moses and gives him these words for living together in peaceful community (Exodus 19–20). The commandments were—and are—a way to respond to the incredible act of God's grace in saving the people from their slavery. When introducing the commandments, God reminds the people: "I am the LORD your God, who brought you out of the land of Egypt, out of the house of slavery" (Exodus 20:2).

The Israelites were called to rely completely on God in the desert, accepting God's salvation and letting God fight their battles. Does God still desire such radical trust on your part? How does it show up in your life?

Shalom is a different way to live. The Ten Commandments are words that, when followed, bring about a community of trust and safety. This is far different from the society the Israelites were accustomed to back in Egypt, and it is a far cry from many of the

Holy war

Many people groups in the ancient world believed that there was a connection between the physical world and the spiritual world, and that people could manipulate their gods into action by performing that same action on earth. This belief influenced their understanding on war. They thought that if they fought wars on earth, then the gods above them would be forced to fight, and once you prompted your gods to fight, you were more likely to win. The Israelites didn't believe this. They looked back to their experience at the Red Sea as the true way of fighting. With the Egyptians hot on their trail, Moses told the people that "the LORD will fight for you, and you have only to keep still" (Exodus 14:14). So, both in the beginning and scattered through the Old Testament, God's people fought wars by trusting in God to act on their behalf. They understood that the Lord did not need them to fight for there to be victory.

Soon after the Red Sea event, the Israelites were tempted to fight for themselves and not trust God for victory in war. They fought the Amalekites while wandering in the wilderness. Rules were developed that helped make war less likely to happen, rules that pushed the Israelites to rely on God and not their own strength. For example, they were not allowed to have a standing army, which kept them from being able to start up a war quickly. They weren't allowed to take anything from the people they conquered, so there wasn't any motive to gain wealth through war. Men couldn't have sex during war times. Sometimes in their attempt to obey God, the Israelites believed that they were to kill everything, even the people they conquered. Did they misunderstand God, the God who called them to bless every family on earth?

The Israelites slipped quickly from the original vision of the Red Sea, where only God fought on their behalf. They moved from fighting with God (Judges 4) to fighting for God (2 Samuel 24), and when they did, they had fewer and fewer successes. They became so unfaithful to God's intent that the prophets said that God actually fought with the Babylonians against them, culminating in the people's exile to Babylon (Jeremiah 21:1–6).

Why is this important? Because Jesus chose to fight evil in the original way. Jesus demonstrated on the cross the most effective way to defeat evil: he submitted himself in obedience to God and let God take care of him. In the short view of things, Jesus' enemies won. They killed him. But in the longer view, Jesus defeated, once and for all, the evil that enslaves us. And God gave him victory through the resurrection.

The apostle Paul understood this original way of fighting evil. He writes in Romans 12:19–21, "Beloved, never avenge yourselves, but leave room for the wrath of God, for it is written, 'Vengeance is mine; I will repay, says the Lord.' Instead, 'if your enemies are hungry, feed them; if they are thirsty, give them something to drink; for by doing this you will heap burning coals on their heads.' Do not be overcome by evil, but overcome evil with good."

Some Christians interpret the stories of God's people fighting in wars in the Old Testament as proof that Christians can fight in wars now. Mennonite Christians, however, believe that followers of Jesus should not fight in any army, but instead, trust God to take care of them. God's intention is for us simply to trust God for protection. Judgment or vengeance belongs to the Lord (Romans 12:19–20). The exodus story is a clear example of this.

Voice A: It's hard to read Leviticus and Numbers. Those books are just a bunch of rules.

Voice B: Yeah, and sometimes it seems like God is a mean judge who is ready to zap us when we don't follow a rule.

Voice C: But is that really being fair to God? Can't the rules have some good purpose?

Michele: I think so, yes, if we understand their historical and cultural contexts. Take the rules about manna, the food God gave the people in the wilderness. The people were told to gather only enough manna for one day's supply. The day before the Sabbath, the people were to gather enough for two days, so that they could truly rest on the Sabbath. That was the rule. If they gathered more than they needed, their precious food supply became worm-filled and unfit to eat. Was this a picky rule from a picky God? No, this rule was in place so they could learn to trust God every day for their food. This rule also underscored the importance of Sabbath rest (see Exodus 16).

communities we live in today. The commandments are words of shalom (the Hebrew word that some translate as peace). It means much more, however, than inward peace with God, or not going to war. To have shalom means to be in right relationship with neighbors. It means everyone has a chance to work and make a decent living, everyone has enough to eat and a house to sleep in. Shalom happens when we are at peace with God, with our inner selves, with one another, and with creation. In that sense, it depicts the world before sin has a chance to break apart those precious relationships.

Shalom enables a different way to worship. By accepting the Ten Commandments the people, in essence, declare God as their ruler. The Israelites, in contrast to all the surrounding cultures, are led and governed by an invisible force. Yes, there was a visible pillar of cloud by day and a pillar of fire by night, but even in this visual display there was a mystery. God was seen and yet hidden. Here in the wilderness God is calling the shots and the people follow. When the pillar starts to move, the people start to move—no questions asked (Numbers 10:11–12).

Even the worship space—the tabernacle—is nothing more than an elaborate tent, ready to follow the Invisible, Almighty Presence (Exodus 26) on the move. This stands in stark contrast to the idol worship and temple system that will later tempt God's people (Jeremiah 7) to think God can be housed in a permanent fixture and manipulated like an ordinary piece of wood (Isaiah 44:9–20). But out in the wilderness, God is free, and God is in control.

The motive for worship is also different. Before knowing the true God, the people prayed to Egyptian gods so they could prosper. If you prayed just the right words in just the right way, the gods were obliged to give you fertile fields and lots of children. But in the wilderness, the Israelites worship God because God acted first to save them. Before they deserved it, God rescued God's people from slavery. Before they deserved it, God provided for their every need. So instead of fearing the gods or working to manipulate the

The Ten Commandments

Then God spoke all these words:

1. I am the LORD your God, who brought you out of the land of Egypt, out of the house of slavery; you shall have no other gods before me.
2. You shall not make for yourself an idol, whether in the form of anything that is in heaven above or that is on the earth beneath or that is in the water under the earth . . .
3. You shall not make wrongful use of the name of the LORD your God, for the LORD will not acquit anyone who misuses his name.
4. Remember the Sabbath day and keep it holy. . . . For in six days the LORD made heaven and earth, the sea, and all that is in them, but rested the seventh day; therefore the LORD blessed the Sabbath day and consecrated it.
5. Honor your father and your mother, so that your days may be long in the land that the LORD your God is giving you.
6. You shall not murder.
7. You shall not commit adultery.
8. You shall not steal.
9. You shall not bear false witness against your neighbor.
10. You shall not covet your neighbor's house; you shall not covet your neighbor's wife, male or female slave, ox, donkey, or anything that belongs to your neighbor.

—Exodus 20:1–4, 7–8, 11–17

Voice A: How many of these stories *actually* happened in history?

Michele: I don't know, but I will say this. Most of the Old Testament was written down hundreds of years after the stories would have happened, and the stories were recorded by Israelites in exile in Babylon (which today is Iraq). Unlike some ancient myths and epics, much of the Bible reads like a historical narrative. The biblical heroes are real people who make mistakes, not superheroes who can do no wrong. It reads like the authors believed the stories really happened. And God is different than mythical deities. God longs for relationship and is willing to be hurt by his people. God refuses to give up on a very stubborn people. You just don't see that kind of loving persistence in the other narratives. I believe the Bible is inspired by God and all those stories *could* have happened because I believe in miracles.

Voice A: So, even if they didn't happen, the stories have a good point?

Michele: Yes. It's also okay to believe these stories happened.

gods, the wilderness people love God. Most people groups of that time recited a statement twice a day in which they reminded themselves out loud some of their most important understandings about their god. These groups tended to say the words *fear god* (using the name of their god). By contrast, the Israelites didn't say the word *fear* but the word *love*. They recited this: "Hear, O Israel: The LORD is our God, the LORD alone. You shall love the LORD your God with all your heart and with all your soul and with all your might" (Deuteronomy 6:4–5; see also Mark 12:29–30).

Shalom requires a different kind of economics. The love and worship of God is also connected to right living (Micah 6:6–8). God wants to form a new society or kingdom where everyone has a chance to experience shalom. God makes a Sabbath for all creation to reflect the rest God took after creation and the rest God gave to those who were enslaved in Egypt. Not only is every seventh day to be a day of rest, but every seven years the ground is to rest from crops and tilling. Every seven years all debts are to be forgiven, and enslaved people are to be set free. These rules give rest to those who have fallen on hard times. And every fifty years, the Jubilee year (Leviticus 25:10), all the land is to be returned to its original owners, thus redistributing wealth. Such a system will level the playing field, while also leaving people free to be productive and industrious. The people obeyed Jubilee as part of their worship of God, who was the real owner of their possessions and land.

Jubilee is an economic system found in Leviticus, in the midst of the stories about the Israelites wandering in the wilderness for forty years. Jubilee rules helped give people second chances to recover from their financial troubles. At the same time, these rules didn't hinder people from working hard and taking initiative.

Voice B: My mom grew up in a conservative church and they were taught to fear God, as in to be afraid of God.

Michele: I think on some level, we've misunderstood Proverbs 9:10–12 where it says that the "fear of the Lord is the beginning of wisdom." We think it means to be afraid of God but really, it's more about respecting God and trusting God with our lives. And we can trust God because God is love.

Voice A: How do we know that God is so loving?

Michele: God lets Abraham haggle with him. That's love. God keeps giving people additional chances, over and over again. That's love. And the fact that sex workers and tax collectors are drawn to Jesus like a magnet. That's love too.

Voice B: So, what does the fear of the Lord mean then?

Michele: It's a bit of a paradox. I think the expression is more about reverence than out and out fear. But on the other hand, God is so holy, so beyond our comprehension, that it can feel a little scary to be in God's presence. It is like standing on top of a mountain, where you experience a mixture of awe and an appropriate level of fear at the grandeur of the mountain. Yet 1 John 4:8 says God is love. Not just loving, but *love.*

Voice A: Somehow, we have to find the happy medium between "Jesus is my Homeboy" and being terrified of God.

Voice B: Yes, well, the Holy Spirit struck down Ananias and Sapphira (Acts 5:1–11) because they only gave half of their income to the church. God is serious business.

Voice A: And yet others like David get forgiven easily.

Voice B: David was sorry for what he did.

Voice A: I think God's hard to understand sometimes.

Taken together, the exodus and wilderness events give us a clear picture of salvation. God rescued people from both physical and spiritual oppression. As Christians, we may look back and say that this salvation was woefully lacking, because *real* salvation has come only with Jesus. But as a Jew, Jesus would have shared a similar understanding of salvation as that depicted in Exodus. He too was concerned about physical and spiritual healing. And, like the exodus–Sinai events, Jesus brought a salvation that is both for the individual and for the people. He gathered twelve disciples around him (Mark 3:13–19); these would be the start of the church, the new people of God.

Why do you worship? What if you know you are supposed to feel thankful and worship God for a particular reason, but you just don't feel like doing it?

Summing it up

- *God begins to solve humanity's sin problem by creating a people.* God calls Abraham and Sarah, whose obedience continues the story of God's work in the world.
- *God calls everyone in one way or another.* We have all been chosen for a mission. That doesn't mean we're God's favorites. It means we have been given a task of bringing God's blessing to the world.
- *God initiates a relationship with us.* God initiated a covenant with Abraham and Sarah and their descendants. God renewed the relationship when God heard the people's cries in Egypt, rescued them from slavery, and formed them into a people. God continued to relate to humanity through Jesus and continues to work through the church and in our lives today.
- *Our worship is a response of love to God.* Worship is not a series of rituals to persuade God to give us favors. This is because God has taken the initiative to act in history.
- *God's people are called to have radical trust in God.* In their escape from Egypt the people of Israel learn they can depend solely on God for protection, rather than fighting their enemies themselves.
- *The people of God are a community founded on shalom.* The Ten Commandments and other Old Testament laws point to God's plan for a society where all have hope, dignity, and a chance to care for themselves economically. Jesus continued this emphasis in his own life and teachings.
- *Salvation is both physical and spiritual, and both individual and collective.* The exodus and wilderness events show that

What will the Israelites do with their newfound freedom? Will it be a quick and easy trip to the Promised Land? And what will God do when things go bad? Read on . . .

God wants to deliver all of our lives from the destructiveness of sin. Jesus also demonstrated this. If sin breaks relationships between God, self, others, and creation, then our salvation brings renewed, healed relationships not only with God, but also with ourselves, others, and creation.

A spiritual discipline to practice

Read Deuteronomy 26:5–10. Rewrite this little story as your own story. You can write about your ancestors (in the spirit of "a wandering Aramean was my ancestor"), a few sentences about troubles

What does salvation mean?

There are many Hebrew (Old Testament) and Greek (New Testament) words that we translate into English as *salvation*. The word *save* in the Old Testament can mean to deliver, bring to safety, redeem, vindicate, help in time of distress, rescue, or set free. Sometimes the meaning of *save* is very specific and individual. Hannah, for example, couldn't have children and was "saved" when God gave her Samuel. Sometimes salvation is more general, as in Psalm 33:19, where the people pray that the Lord will save Israel from famine and death.

Salvation in the Old Testament can mean physical or spiritual deliverance (see Ezekiel 36:22–32; 37:1–14; Jeremiah 31:31–34), but it is always clear that it comes from God, not from some natural event or human force (Psalm 33:16–17).

The most commonly used word in the New Testament for salvation means to save and to heal. Jesus used the same word when he said, "Your faith has made you well" (Mark 10:52; Luke 17:19) that he used to say, "Your faith has saved you" (Luke 7:50). As in the Old Testament, there is more than one layer of meaning to stories and words. When Peter walks on the water, he cries to Jesus to save him (Matthew 14:22–33). On one level, Peter needs to be saved physically from drowning, but it's also obvious from the story that Peter needs to be rescued spiritually from his doubt and fear.

Throughout the Bible, salvation is experienced as people trust God (Psalm 22:4). We are "saved by faith" through God's initiative, not our own efforts, even though salvation motivates us to respond with "good works" (Ephesians 2:8–10). God's saving work in our lives motivates us to love, caring for the poor and oppressed (Leviticus 19:33; Deuteronomy 10:18–19).

Salvation leads to changed behavior. Jesus tells the woman caught in adultery, "Neither do I condemn you. Go your way, and from now on do not sin again" (John 8:11). Touched by Jesus' visit to his house, Zacchaeus volunteers to give back the money he took from people. "Today salvation has come to this house," Jesus replies (Luke 19:9).

you have experienced, and then record how God rescued you in the past or is rescuing you right now. Finally, you can write about your new "land flowing with milk and honey" and about what you are going to do in response to God's rescue ("now I bring the first of the fruit of the ground"). If you don't think you have begun to feel God's rescue, you can write about that instead.

Covenant

God did what it took to create a people who would learn how to love and trust God and live in a peaceful, just community with each other. One of the specific ways God helped them understand such relationships was through covenants. In much the same way that ancient rulers made political alliances with each other or with their subjects, God made covenants with people. Some were unconditional, where God promised blessings no matter what. Others were conditional, where God promised to bless the people if they were faithful.

Here are some of the main covenants in the Bible:

- Noah (Genesis 8:21–22; 9:8–17)
- Abraham (Genesis 12:1–3; 15:4–20; 17:2–8)
- Sinai Covenant through Moses (Exodus 19:3–6; 20:1–17)
- Shechem Covenant through Joshua (Joshua 24)
- David (2 Samuel 7:11b–16)
- Jeremiah's vision of a new covenant (Jeremiah 31:31–34)
- Ezekiel's vision of a new covenant (Ezekiel 36)
- Ezra's covenant renewal (Nehemiah 10:28–31)
- Jesus' new covenant (Matthew 26:28; Mark 14:24; Luke 22:20)

These covenants established a relationship between God and people. While each party had to hold up its end of the bargain, only God initiated the covenant. Often, we read that God stayed with the covenant agreement even when the people failed to do their part (Isaiah 54:10). Sometimes God was so hurt by what the people did that God considered starting all over again with a new people (for example, Exodus 32). But each time, the people or their leaders would plead with God and then God decided to stick with the chosen people. In the Old Testament, this is called God's "steadfast love." In the wilderness, the Israelites rebelled, and Moses asked the Lord to forgive the people according to steadfast love, which God does (Numbers 14:7–19). Steadfast love can also describe God's active love in non-covenantal situations. Jonah was mad at God because the Lord showed steadfast love to the Ninevites, a people group Jonah believed was beyond deserving forgiveness (Jonah 4:1–4). Jesus illustrated this marvelous type of love in the story of the Prodigal Son, where the father forgives and welcomes back a son who dishonors him (Luke 15:11–32). Other New Testament examples of mercy include Matthew 9:13 and 12:13.

TOPICS IN CHAPTER 3

- Faith as a long journey
- The temptation to be like others
- How we read the Bible
- God as the only true ruler
- Judgment is also grace—new starts
- Keeping pure in a dirty world

STORYLINE

- Israelites in the wilderness
- Entering the Promised Land
- Judges and kings
- Israel in exile
- Rebuilding Jerusalem

3. Competing Gods

Okay, we're at the Promised Land. Can we go home now?

IT WOULD SEEM, AT FIRST GLANCE, that all is well. The Israelites have been saved from slavery in Egypt and are being saved from enslaved thinking in the wilderness. What was once a crowd has become a people, birthed at the Red Sea with a simple path forward. The people can trust God for all their needs, worship God out of love and gratitude, and live in a shalom justice community.

If only they could! The Israelites make many mistakes along the way. The old ways of being, thinking, and living are hard to give up. The new way of obeying an invisible Presence who doesn't function like the Egyptian gods is frustrating, scary, and sometimes downright mystifying. And God's people mess up—miserably.

Voice A: Why forty years in the wilderness?

Voice B: Isn't the exodus and the wilderness like our own experience? I always thought that as soon as I got baptized, I'd go straight to the Promised Land. Everything would be great. I thought I would never be tempted again.

Voice C: I've heard people say that Satan tempts you more after you are baptized.

Michele: No one told me to expect that phenomenon, but I experienced that and it really threw me. I doubted my baptism for a while.

Voice B: Maybe there's more to Christianity than just getting into heaven.

Voice C: Actually, if you really look at the stories of Jesus, you know there's more to it.

God takes the long road

As in our own lives, faith was a journey for the Israelites. The Israelites did manage to reach the border of the Promised Land, but sadly, they couldn't go in. They could have gone in, had they had faith enough to trust that God would take care of them. Twelve spies go into the land and see that it is incredibly fertile, "flowing with milk and honey." But, said ten of them, the people there are giants and the cities fortified. Who were they to go against those kinds of odds? The ten advise the people that their entry would be disastrous. The other two spies, Joshua and Caleb, say that with God's help they can enter. Was this not the same God who rescued them at the Red Sea, who gave them manna every day, who led them by the mysterious pillar of cloud and fire? How many miraculous events do they need? (See Numbers 13–14 for the whole story.)

Judgment is the grace again. In the end, the ten doubters win out, and God tells the people that for their lack of faith they will now have to wander the desert for forty more years. But as before, God's judgment is also the grace. The people need a stretch of time to figure out who their God, Yahweh, is. They need time to learn to trust God fully. During these forty years, God will continue to re-form this infant people. God knows Canaan will be filled with plenty of its own new challenges.

syncretism: *gradually mixing two religions together so that you are practicing both*

We can look down on the Israelites for their idol worship, but we also need to admit we let a lot of "other gods" mix with our own faith. Consider God and country. God and the gun. God and consumerism. Yet we can't be totally separate from our culture either. At what point is the mixing of our culture and faith wrong? When you start to oppress people. When you begin to domesticate God. When you put labels on God as a way to control God. Isn't that what idol worship is?

Finally, a new home opens. After forty years and the death of Moses, the Israelites enter Canaan, the Promised Land, under the leadership of Joshua (Joshua 3–4). They conquer many areas, but not all of them. So instead of settling on land that has no other occupants, they settle among peoples who have different understandings about the divine world (Joshua 17:16–18; Judges 2:1–3; 3:4).

The inhabitants of Canaan rely upon gods called Baals to grant them survival through good harvests and many children. The Israelites are used to herding sheep in the solitary wilderness. New neighbors and new agricultural demands put pressure on them to adopt Baal worship. The pressure is immense and the Israelites give in. They combine Yahweh worship with Baal worship, hoping that idol worship will cause their crops to grow (Judges 10:6). They abandon God's ethics of living in a shalom community. The people even began to give their children Baal names, just to be on the safe side (Judges 8:33–35). And this gradual mixing of two religions, called syncretism, became their undoing (Jeremiah 7:16–8:3).

God's steadfast love persists. Israel's merciful and holy God refuses to give up on the people. This time God provides judges—leaders who administer government under God. As the book of Judges tells it, a predictable cycle occurs under these leaders:

1. The Israelites fail to live up to the promises they made to God.
2. This sin brings about oppression, as God allows other groups to capture the Israelites and rule them with an iron hand.
3. In desperation, the Israelites cry out to God.
4. Moved by their pleas, God acts by appointing a judge to lead them.
5. The judge helps deliver the Israelites through a modified holy war (see p. 51). Even more important, the judge reminds them of the exodus and God's gracious leading and providence.
6. As soon as the judge dies, the people forget. They forget God and they forget the Story. They slip back into their old ways (see Judges 3–4 for examples).

The Israelites want a king. The up and down cycle of the judges gets old, so the Israelites ask one of their judges, Samuel, to anoint a human ruler for them as king. Enemies were threatening invasion, and Samuel's own sons were rotten judges. Additionally, all the peoples around the Israelites had kings. Samuel, however, remembers the wilderness dream that God would be their king. He asks God what he should do. "They have not rejected you," says God, "but they have rejected me from being king over them" (1 Samuel 8:7).

Getting rid of the Canaanites

Voice A: I don't like the idea that God told the Israelites to get rid of all the Canaanites. If we're chosen for a mission to bless all people, then this kind of destruction is a major detour. So, did the people just *think* God told them that?

Voice B: You can't make the Bible say things it doesn't say just because you're uncomfortable with it.

Voice A: Yeah, but they didn't have Jesus yet, so I think they misunderstood God—a lot.

Michele: What's sad for me is that thousands of years later, the church used this narrative to justify the Doctrine of Discovery, a ruling that gave European Christians who visited unfamiliar lands the right to kill native peoples.

Voice B: That doesn't look like Jesus.

Michele: Throughout the Bible, there is a tension between staying away from other peoples because they might tempt you away from God (syncretism) and our call to mingle with other peoples so that God may bless them through us. And this tension never resolves. The Canaanites' idol worship threatened the Israelites' ability to be faithful, and yet I don't think that's a good enough reason to kill an entire people group. And many non-Israelites joined God's people and were faithful.

This is why we have to focus on Jesus' words and actions to guide us when other parts of the Bible seem to justify evil.

Samuel warns the people that human kings will abuse their power, tax the people, take their best fields and crops, and eventually enslave the Israelites' sons and daughters. But his words fall on deaf ears: the Israelites still demand a human king. Samuel goes back to God, who now instructs him to do what the people want. (See 1 Samuel 8 for the whole story.)

This sets up an interesting problem for us today. What *was* God's will for the people? Did it matter to God whether they had a human king? Or did God really want them to have a king all along? And why didn't God simply force them into obedience or perform some incredible miracle to prove that they were safe and secure with Yahweh, God, as their only king?

These questions are all the more complicated and important because the book of 1 Samuel records two different reactions to monarchy. In the anti-monarchy strand (1 Samuel 8; 10:17–27;

12), God pronounces judgment on the people for choosing a king. Saul, the first king to be anointed, is shown to be a bumbling fool. In the pro-monarchy strand (1 Samuel 9:1–10:16; 10:27b–11:15), Saul is filled with divine spirit so that he prophesies and leads the Israelites in successful holy war. He even spares the lives of those who speak against him. So which strand is right? (See the sidebar "When the Bible story comes in different versions." See also "Tips on using the Bible to guide your decision-making" on p. 173.)

When the Bible seems to contradict itself

Many people find it upsetting that the Bible sometimes carries two strands of the same story. What does this mean? Is one strand right and the other wrong? Does this mean the Bible is not God's inspired word?

It helps to understand how stories functioned in the ancient world. Back then, historical accuracy was viewed differently than it is today. It was important to communicate the essence of a story, using the facts to lift out the symbolism and special meaning of the bigger story. The New Testament writer John, for example, put the story of Jesus chasing the moneychangers from the temple at the beginning of Jesus' ministry; the gospels of Matthew, Mark, and Luke put it near the end. John was not as concerned about when the event actually happened as he was about conveying the true meaning of the temple. Since one of John's main themes in the gospel is that Jesus, not the temple, is the center of faith, he chose to tell that story at the beginning.

Most of the stories in the Old Testament were passed on by word of mouth for hundreds of years before they were written down on animal skins or papyrus. Story was so important to the people's identity that when slightly different versions of the same story would emerge—which was likely when so many different groups recited the same story from memory instead of a written record—the Hebrews kept both stories. Instead of declaring one right and the other one wrong, the stories were considered so sacred that the editors would often place them side by side in the text. They trusted that there was something special in each story; they didn't trust themselves to judge which story was more "true."

When we view Christian scripture in this way, we can still trust the Bible as inspired by God. The stories exist in creative tension with each other, speaking to each other as well as to us. We need to love the Bible enough to study it, identify and talk about the different strands that coexist, and use the whole message of the Bible, particularly the life and teachings of Jesus, to help us determine God's will.

Read the Confession of Faith summary of Article 4 about Scripture on page 183.

The people see how God reigns. In Samuel's day, God wanted to be the only ruler, so God could lead them along the right path. But the people wanted to have a human king to be like the nations around them. God could have forced the people to fall into line under divine kingship. Instead, in love and mercy, God gave them free choice. And they chose to have a human king. God eventually worked out divine purposes through the royal line of David. This kind of thing happens in story after story in the Bible. God has a Plan A, the people choose another way, and God moves to Plan B.

When have you been aware that God gives you free choice?

How do we know that God's direct rule was God's best plan and that the monarchy was God's second choice? We don't know for sure, but we can look at what happened in the story. The monarchy helped shape the Israelites' false idea that God belonged only to their nation. It nurtured the idea that God can only be found and worshiped in a certain place: their temple. The change happened slowly, and there were a few shining examples of godly kings. But little by little, the God who used to set the agenda in the wilderness became the God who was used to bless the government of the day. The God who used to be worshiped anywhere became the God who could only be found in the temple.

Can you think of a time in your life when you realized you didn't choose God's original plan for you and so God began working out a plan B in your life?

When God was king in the wilderness, the intended jubilee system made sure everyone had enough and that no one was allowed to hoard or be greedy. But under the monarchy, the economic system meant abundance and wealth for some and poverty for others. King Solomon heavily taxed his own people as he built the temple and expanded his own wealth (1 Kings 4:7–19, 22–28; 12:1–14).

Leadership was different, too. In the wilderness, Moses worked with the people to create a free community of shalom. The Israelite

Voice A: Why can't we add things to the Bible?

Michele: Because the controversy about what is authoritative and what is not would be endless. That's why.

Voice B: Isn't it controversial already?

Michele: There was an intentional process for compiling both the Old and New Testaments; certain writings were considered authoritative, and these writings were canonized, meaning that that the church leaders decided these writings should become *the* book—the Bible—and that all other writings would be measured by the Bible. Before the Bible became canonized, the church as a gathered body had authority over the writings, but after this process, the Bible had authority over the church.

Voice A: But what if the ancient church leaders got it wrong?

Michele: I guess we have to trust that the Holy Spirit inspired those leaders—or tried to—as much as the Spirit inspired the actual writers. I think we have to accept what people decided fifteen hundred years ago because Jesus isn't here to weigh in.

Voice B: But in one sense, he is. The Holy Spirit is the Spirit of Jesus, right?

Michele: I think you're right, and if that's true, then is the Bible the Word of God? Or is it the testament to the Word of God? Or is the Word of God Jesus himself (John 1:1)? Is the Word the Bible or the Spirit moving among us? Remember, there are stories in the Bible where the Spirit claims authority over the Old Testament scriptures (Acts 10). So, can't the Spirit do that with the New Testament?

Voice A: Yes, but that opens up a can of worms.

Michele: Even if it does, if it's the truth, then we need to live into that truth.

kings, by contrast, acted a lot like the pagan kings in the surrounding countries. They oppressed their own people and used religion to justify their actions (Jeremiah 34:8–22). Because they had the temple, the kings assumed God was on their side (Jeremiah 7:1–15). The people put more and more faith in their military power than in God doing the fighting for them.

In the end, Samuel's warnings all came true and the kingdom crumbled. Shalom was rare under the Israelite kings. It's no surprise, then, that when Jesus came, he identified himself with the prophets more than his kingly ancestors. It was Elijah and Moses who met him on the Mount of Transfiguration, not David and Solomon (Luke 9:28–36). This encounter suggests again that while

See the Confession of Faith summary of Article 23 about church and government on page 185.

Are you more comfortable with the God of the wilderness or the God that the monarchy represented? What happens when you only emphasize one revelation of God instead of the other?

God sometimes works through human government, our fundamental allegiance must be to God alone.

shalom justice:
when people get what they need instead of the bad consequences they deserve[5]

The prophets keep the vision alive

Even though things have gone wrong in so many ways, God keeps planning for the people's good. Now, instead of judges, God raises up prophets. These men and women speak God's word, especially to the ones in power. They "comfort the afflicted and afflict the comfortable." They confront the kings when they forget about shalom justice for all (Amos 2:6–16; 4). They rail against idol worship (1 Kings 18). They champion the cause of the poor (Jeremiah 5:26–29; Amos 8:4–8).

Over and over again, the prophets remind the people of the Story—especially the exodus—and hold up the vision of shalom (for example, Amos 9:11-15) and who God is. As a result, they are often persecuted for that vision (Jeremiah 37–38). In many ways, the prophets reflect the kind of ministry Jesus had. Although Jesus was "king," he was a servant whose life and teachings were more in line with the prophets' vision of God than the kings' vision.

How we see Jesus, how we see ourselves

How we view the Story in the Old Testament affects how we view Jesus and how we believe and act as Christians. If a monarchy was what God really desired, then our picture of Jesus would tend to emphasize Jesus as a militant king, and it would be easy to justify a faith that mixes esteem of God, wealth, and country in equal measure. But if the experience of God in the wilderness represents God's ideal, then we can more easily see Jesus as a servant king who comes to restore shalom to a community where everyone can follow God and no country is God's favorite. God's people solve problems nonviolently by trusting in God, not in money or military power. God's people take their cues from the economic principles of Jubilee, where we voluntarily share what we have so that all may have shalom.

The kingdom divides

Despite the prophets preaching God's word to the people, the troubles continue for the people of God. Israel's united monarchy lasted only one hundred years and three kings. By King Solomon's time, only four hundred years after being freed from slavery in Egypt, the people are enslaved by their own making. And now the kingdom divides in two. The ten northern tribes, Israel, revolt against the two southern tribes, Judah and Benjamin, where the king and Jerusalem are housed.

The division does not bring either nation any closer to God. Both struggle with Baal worship and social injustice (1 Kings 16:29–34; 21:1–9). Both stubbornly believe that God is only their God and can only be found in their territory. Even the reforms led by Kings Hezekiah and Josiah of Judah (2 Kings 18 and 22) are not enough to stave off the judgment of God. Israel falls to Assyria in 722 BCE and the ten northern tribes are dispersed and lost from history. Judah falls to the Babylonians in 587 BCE.

Baals

Other peoples who surrounded the Israelites worshiped gods that the Bible calls Baals. Baal worshipers saw these gods as beings who lived above the sky, who could be influenced by just the right prayers and rituals. In one sense, these Baals had to do their part when the humans did theirs. Yahweh, the Lord, was very different. Yahweh stepped into history, taking the initiative to rescue the enslaved people from Pharaoh. God was not manipulated into saving the Israelites. God loved them. Likewise, the Israelites were instructed to worship God not in order to receive special favors, but out of thankfulness for God's acts of love.

God's judgment leads to grace

The people of Judah are taken into exile in Babylon and remain there for somewhere between fifty to seventy years. This is especially painful, but it is very important to their survival as a people. While living in Babylon, they realize that God doesn't have to be worshiped only at the temple. They begin to meet in smaller groups called synagogues, and many participate more fully in worship than they did back in Jerusalem. Without the temple the people rediscover the Torah or Law (now our first five books of the Bible) and other sacred writings. In order to preserve their identity, they collect, organize, and write down more of their story. Since they come from the land of Judah and most of them are from the tribe of Judah, they start to become known as Jews. In all these ways the people of God are being strengthened in the midst of painful circumstances. They rediscover their identity as they rediscover the Story.

When in your life has judgment gone together with grace?

A second exodus occurs

After the Persians conquer the Babylonians, the people of God are allowed to return home. In some ways, it feels like a second exodus (Jeremiah 16:14–15). As in the first exodus, the people

Voice A: I think it's dangerous to say suffering is redemptive.

Voice B: And by that, do you mean to say that suffering can be good?

Voice A: Yes. If you say that suffering can be good, then you can justify all sorts of violence, bullying, or other painful things. You can even let God off the hook by saying, "Well, God let that awful event happen to build your character."

Michele: I agree we need to be careful here when we respond to people in the throes of grief and loss. I would never say things like "God's trying to build your faith," or "Everything happens for a reason." We must watch our words when an individual is going through a tough time. And I don't think God works that way necessarily.

Voice A: Sometimes suffering happens to a person because other people sin and are mean-spirited. They're jerks.

Voice C: Then why doesn't God stop the jerks?

Voice B: Because then God would end up stopping all of us. We're all jerks, at least some of the time.

Voice C: So then if God lets us suffer because we're jerks, then suffering is redemptive.

Michele: Actually, if God stopped all evil, then God would also be messing with your free will—that is, your freedom to choose what you want to do. So yes, bad things happen because humans have free will and there are consequences. And sometimes you're making the right choice, but someone else isn't—and the result hurts you. I don't know why God sometimes steps in and rescues people and sometimes seems completely absent. I also believe God is with us and loving us even when it doesn't feel that way. I think that suffering is sometimes—and only sometimes—redemptive when we look at whole people groups, like the exiles living in Babylon. The exile was so painful for an entire group of people, but it also disrupted the wrong ideas the Israelites had about God being only their national God. The exile brought spiritual renewal.

And we have to remember that God doesn't let suffering, even redemptive suffering, happen forever. Think about how God comforted the people of Israel in Isaiah 40.

have another chance to really live out the ideals of the wilderness experience. And to a certain extent, things are better. Sabbath and other aspects of worshiping God take on greater meaning. Worshiping God through right living continues to be a challenge (Isaiah 58), and there is an ongoing need to learn to trust God for everything. People study Torah, God's law, in order to find out how to live rightly.

In several ways, however, they fall short. Perhaps their greatest dilemma is deciding how to be the chosen people who will bless others. Back in Jerusalem, the small percentage of Jews who were not exiled had intermarried with other peoples. When the exiled Jews return to Judah, they have to decide what to do about the foreign spouses and children. Ezra leads a reform, calling for all Jews to get rid of the foreigners.

On the one hand, Ezra is concerned for purity (Ezra 9:1–4). Some parts of the law forbade the marrying of foreigners (Exodus 34:15–16; Deuteronomy 7:3–4), and Ezra really wants to obey God. That concern for honoring God is something we can admire. On the other hand, Ezra excludes people from worshiping God solely because of their bloodline. Had he only been concerned about syncretism, he would have asked the people if they were willing to follow Yahweh, and if they said yes, then they could have joined God's people. But Ezra only asks the ethnic question; he doesn't give the foreign spouses a chance to say yes to following God. He seems to forget moments when foreigners *were* included in the Story—including many who were enslaved, who came out of Egypt with the Israelites, and non-Israelite

---

Voice A: Do we have a subtle version of Ezra's problem, what I'd call ethnocentrism? That's when we say "I'm a Mennonite Christian [or another category], so I'm the best." How does that feel if you're Catholic, or even Muslim?

Michele: I agree that it would be ethnocentric if I think I'm a Mennonite because of my ethnicity. But that's not at all what the first Mennonites wanted. Their big focus was to communicate that everyone is a first-generation Christian; in other words, everyone must choose for themselves whether to have a relationship with Jesus regardless of ethnic background.

Voice B: I think it's okay to discern different theological views. Isn't that what we're doing right now? And I think it's okay to make choices about which understandings about God and Jesus are the best.

Michele: Right, and that's not judging people because of their race. Anyone can choose to love Jesus.

Voice A: But whenever we have theological conversations with people who disagree with us, we must first have a real relationship with them. We have to care for them as persons or we aren't really following Jesus, even if we have the best understanding of truth.

women like Rahab and Ruth, who married Israelites and became ancestors of the kings. He forgets what Abraham and all his descendants were chosen to do—to bless every family on earth (Genesis 12:3).

The Old Testament story ends with many of these struggles remaining and many questions unresolved. But look at the ground we've covered: God's people broke their part of the covenant many times. They forgot the vision of God revealed in the wilderness. They mixed the worship of God with worship of other gods. Yet God remained faithful. God sent judges, and later on, prophets. God worked with less than perfect situations, such as the monarchy. When the people truly became desperate, God rescued them. And even God's judgment on them in exile—their loss of independence as other nations took over them—became a blessing in disguise.

After the exile, the people of God started yearning more and more for a new kind of leader, a leader who would finally help them stay completely faithful to God. They called this leader the messiah, or "the anointed one." Sometimes they proclaimed a human leader as a temporary messiah, such as the Persian king Cyrus, when he defeated Babylon and allowed the Jews to return to their homeland (Isaiah 45:1). At other times, they looked forward to a time when God would send someone special who would be the final messiah (Isaiah 42; 49; 61). When would the messiah come? What would he be like? That's what the next chapter is about.

Summing it up

- *God has an ultimate plan but stays with us when we choose the wrong way.* God gives us free choice, and sometimes we make choices that show a lack of faith (like the Israelites turning back from entering Canaan the first time or choosing a human king). Such choices bring painful consequences, but judgment often calls us to better things.

- *God sends people to help us be faithful.* In the Bible, God sends judges and prophets to remind the people of God's way. The message was often unpopular, but when the people of God listened, things improved significantly.

- *Syncretism, the combined worship of God and idols, is detrimental to our faith.* The Israelites were tempted to worship both Yahweh and idols just to be on the safe side. We also compromise our faith by mixing it with values of dominant culture, such as greed or consumerism or nationalism. At the same time, God calls us to love and welcome others, even those with differing values from ours.

- *God is with us even in the most difficult of times.* When the people of Judah and Israel went into exile, it really felt like the bottom had dropped out of their world. But God was there. God uses painful experiences to bring us back to where we should be.

- *How we see the Bible helps determine how we view Jesus and understand our lives as Christians.* These God-inspired stories in the Bible tell us what did happen, not necessarily what should have happened. From the whole mix, we must figure out who God really is and how to be faithful to God.

A spiritual discipline to practice

There are many situations in our lives that request our ultimate trust. A big part of being a Christian is to dare to trust God over everything and everyone else. Take some time to think about what and whom you are tempted to trust instead of trusting God when times get tough for you. Write out a list of these things and people who function as Baals in your life. Do you ever mix "gods"? Or, in other words, do you say you trust in God but you also rely on this person or that idea, just in case?

After reflecting on your Baals, write a letter to God. Will you ask for forgiveness, for help to trust God more, to see God's power more, or maybe all of the above? What will you write?

TOPICS IN CHAPTER 4

- God comes in human form
- Jesus: a different kind of Messiah
- Jubilee living from the heart
- Good news for all, even enemies
- Words, actions, and salvation
- A call to follow

STORYLINE

- Jesus is born
- Jesus' works of healing and teaching

4. Enter Jesus

MANY PEOPLE IN FIRST-CENTURY PALESTINE wanted a messiah—someone God would send to deliver the people from their oppression. Life in the Roman Empire was brutal. Many people were taxed to the point of starvation. Some sold themselves or their children into slavery. Troublemakers were crucified. When the Romans said, "Jump!" the Jews asked, "How high?" This was the world Jesus was born into—politically charged, unsafe streets, lots of poor people. The future looked bleak.

The Jews remembered God's miraculous action in the exodus; they longed again for deliverance. Some Jews longed for a military solution, and others longed for another Moses who would promote such radical obedience that God would surely rescue them. But all wanted the same thing: to get rid of the Romans.

Voice A: If we're going to question or deconstruct every single thing about Jesus, I'm out.

Michele: It's important to ask the hard questions.

Voice A: Yes, but at what point is doing so causing more damage than good? Maybe I don't care about whether the miracles *actually* happened.

Michele: I hear you. Humans can't totally understand God or Jesus, and if we try to do so anyway, that's arrogant. But some of us must ask the questions because they're burning up inside us. And some of us just need his help to press on when we don't have all the answers.

Jesus: a humble birth in a lousy location

Jesus was born to a carpenter and his wife, natives of the northern region of Galilee. They gave him a name that was as common in Galilee as Bob is in the United States, and after his birth in Bethlehem they lived in a seemingly insignificant, out-of-the-way town. No government parade on the day of his arrival. No religious escort to the temple. Jesus was born among the cows because there was no room in the main area of the house (or "inn," as tradition would have it). And rumors floated through the village that he was an illegitimate child. Jesus had very humble beginnings (Matthew 1:18–25; Mark 6:3; Luke 2).

In as many ways as Jesus' birth was common, it was also uncommon. He was conceived supernaturally in the womb of a virgin (Luke 1:26–38). Royal astrologers from the East came to pay him homage (Matthew 2:1–12). So did shepherds, people considered too unclean to worship in the synagogue because of their occupation (Luke 2:8–20). In some ways Jesus was totally unknown, but in other ways he was known too well. Herod wanted to kill him so much that he had all the infant boys in Bethlehem slaughtered (Matthew 2:16–18).

Voice A: They named him Bob? Isn't that disrespectful?

Michele: I don't mean to be. Of all the names in the world, "Jesus" is perfect because it means "Yahweh [the Lord] saves." And because of who Jesus is, that name holds such special meaning. Yet many other little boys were called Yeshua (Jesus) in Jesus' day. As a human, Jesus experienced everything that we have experienced (Hebrews 4:15). See, this is the incarnation. Totally God, but at the same time totally human, even to the point of having a common name.

Jesus: a life outside the box

What Jesus does for the next thirty years, except for his trip to the temple at age twelve (Luke 2:41–52), is left out of the gospel accounts. The Gospels pick up the story when the adult Jesus asks his cousin John to baptize him (Luke 3:21–22). John is calling the Jews to repent—to turn around and change their sinful behaviors and attitudes. Jesus didn't sin (Hebrews 4:15), yet he asks

incarnation:
God taking on human form in Jesus Christ

Voice A: Why do we have this story of the virgin birth?

Michele: Matthew and Luke had no good motive for including the story in their writings—unless it was true. The pagan religions of that day had similar stories about god-heroes who were born of a woman who had been impregnated by a god. Why would the Christians have risked including this similarity to paganism unless the virgin birth was true and supported their message that Jesus was the Son of God?[6] I agree that it's hard to believe sometimes—maybe it feels impossible. And perhaps the virgin birth is intended to function as a metaphor for Jesus' special connection to God. We can't know for sure. I believe that miracles can and do happen, though, and I believe that God loves us even when we find it hard to believe.

for baptism. Why? Surely Jesus wanted to be an example for the people then and for us today, but perhaps something more was going on.

As John baptizes Jesus, a voice speaks from heaven: "You are my Son, the Beloved; with you I am well pleased" (Luke 3:22). The quote contains two fragments of scripture that had special meaning for the Jews. "You are my Son, the Beloved" comes from Psalm 2:7, which was used whenever a king was enthroned as the new ruler. "With you I am well pleased" is a part of Isaiah's prophecy about a suffering servant (Isaiah 42:1). Put together, these quotes send a message to Jesus and to the crowd about who Jesus is. Jesus is a king, a servant king (Luke 3:21–22).

What kind of Messiah? Jesus has to reflect on what God is calling him to do as Messiah. So he heads for the wilderness for forty days (Luke 4:1–13). There, Satan (or the devil) offers ideas about what kind of king Jesus can be. Satan gives Jesus three offers. The first is for Jesus to satisfy his hunger by turning rocks into bread. After all, Jesus hasn't eaten in forty days. Satan then offers him all the political power in the world if Jesus will just bow down and worship the devil. Finally, Satan takes Jesus to the top of the temple. There Satan reminds him that angels will not let him be hurt, and he can prove that by jumping off the pinnacle.

What could hurt? What's wrong with turning rocks into bread? Didn't Jesus do something similar when he fed the five thousand (Luke 9:10–17)? If he had political and military power he could "gently persuade" the whole world to worship God. And what a great idea to demonstrate God's power by jumping off the temple roof and landing without harm! That would impress people.

Q: Does anyone else see the connection between Pharaoh killing all the baby boys during the time of Moses and now King Herod killing all the baby boys in Bethlehem?

A: Yes! The first time God is rescuing his people out of Egypt and this time, Mary and Joseph are fleeing to Egypt.

It's mind-boggling to think of Jesus as both fully God and fully human. If you only see Jesus as God (and therefore fully divine), then his death on the cross probably doesn't mean much to you, because you might think he wouldn't have felt any pain. And by fixating on the divinity of Jesus, you might downplay his ethical teachings and focus mostly on the miracles. On the flip side, if you only see Jesus as human, then you might downplay Jesus' miracles, especially his resurrection. So even though it's hard to understand, we have to hold onto this tension.

No, the temptations were not so terrible in themselves. The larger issue at stake was what kind of messiah Jesus would be. Forcing people in any way to believe Jesus was the Messiah—either by economic incentives, military power, or by wowing them with miracles—was not God's way.

There were times when Jesus did these very things. He provided fish for people's physical hunger (Luke 5:1–11; Mark 5:21–43). He performed many miracles (Matthew 12:9–14), but he often told people who were healed not to broadcast the news of their healing (Mark 3:7–12). He refused to do miracles when people wanted "proof" of his power (see Mark 8:11–12). Jesus knew that if he became an economic, wonder-working, or military messiah, then the people would not follow him out of love. He also knew that if he became any of these messiahs, he could avoid what he knew lay ahead of him, what lies ahead for anyone who follows God fully. He could avoid suffering. He could avoid the cross—that was the real temptation.

Q: The military Messiah sounds like what Christians did in the Crusades, right? (For more on the Crusades, see p. 163.) The church caved in to the very temptations to force shalom on earth that Jesus said no to when the devil tempted him (see Luke 4:1–13).

A: Yes, and it can happen today too.

But to that temptation, Jesus says no. He says no to tricking or forcing people to follow him. He says no to the easy way to power. And in doing so, he says yes to suffering.

Being tempted isn't sin in itself. It's saying yes and giving in to temptation that's wrong. Many new Christians struggle with this concept. They think they're terrible and displeasing to God because they field many temptations in their minds. But everyone faces temptations. The problem comes only when we yield to them.

Jubilee for everyone. Having decided what kind of messiah he would *not* be, Jesus now has to announce what kind of messiah he *will* be. He heads for Nazareth, the town where he had grown up (Luke 4:16–30). There, at a synagogue service, he reads from the scroll of Isaiah. "The Spirit of the Lord is upon me, because he has anointed me to bring good news to the poor. He has sent me to proclaim release to the captives and recovery of sight to the blind, to set free those who are oppressed, to proclaim the year of the Lord's favor" (Luke 4:18–19). The year of the Lord's favor is a nod to the Jubilee economics of the wilderness.

When he sits down, every eye is fixed on him. "Today this scripture has been fulfilled in your hearing," he says (Luke 4:21). Now they are amazed. Isn't this Joseph's son from down the street? But there is something in his voice that gives them the feeling that the jubilee he read about would soon be theirs. They have been longing for these very prophecies to come true. This is wonderful news.

Jesus takes this good news a step further. He speaks of the prophets helping Gentiles. Jesus reminds the hearers about the time when the prophet Elijah saved the widow of Zarephath from starvation (1 Kings 17:8–24), and then he tells them about the prophet Elisha healing Naaman the Syrian from leprosy (2 Kings 5:1–19).

Voice A: Does God love the Gentiles? Aren't the Jews, in a way, God's favorites?

Michele: Good question. Let's be clear that God *does* love the Jewish people very much. I think God gave them a special job to do: to be the context and the people out of which Jesus emerges. It's a both/and situation. I see a thread that runs through the entire biblical narrative. The thread? That God chooses us to work through humans—first the Jews, then Christians—to show everyone else they are chosen as God's beloved too. And once you see the thread, you can't un-see it.

Voice A: Okay, so why didn't the people in the Bible see it? Hmm, to answer my own question, I think we can make the same mistake today. Rather, we do make the same mistake today. We cave to the temptation to think we're God's favorites.

Voice B: Or what if Michele is wrong, or just making excuses for God to make him look better? How do you know you're right?

Michele: I'll never be sure I'm one hundred percent right about anything. But to help me get closer to the truth, I choose to look at issues through the lens of Jesus. Jesus loved and interacted with Gentiles, women, societal outcasts—all the people deemed unclean in their world.

Voice A: What makes you confident that God is real? How can I believe when my prayers are not answered?

Michele: I'll say this gently because I know others have asked for miracles and they haven't received them yet. I've seen physical miracles, though, like my sister being healed of a hole in her heart. Better yet, I've seen Jesus at work in the world today. People sense him telling them to do this or that, they follow Jesus' prompting, and someone is rescued as a result. I know I'm fortunate in this regard. And again, once you see God at work, you can't un-see it. In this case, I don't ever want to.

This good news—freedom for the captives, sight for the blind, food for the poor—is God's desire for non-Israelites as well as Israelites. This good news, Jesus says, is not only for the Jews. God has always intended it for every person, every people, every race.

Now they want to kill him. The people who admired him only moments before become so angry they try to hurl him off a cliff. The wonderful hometown boy is suddenly a threat. Jesus dares to contradict their treasured belief that they are God's favorite people? Jesus dares to challenge Ezra's notion (see p. 71) that God wanted a people of God that excluded Gentiles? The widow of Zarephath was from Phoenicia. Naaman was a military captain from Syria. God sent prophets to help these two people, who were Gentiles and part of enemy countries. And this made the people of Nazareth mad!

Good news for the whole person. The very things Jesus read at the synagogue in Nazareth, he made into reality.

- Jesus healed physical diseases.
- He spoke against economic injustice and told the rich not to hoard their wealth (Luke 18–19). He brought the year of Jubilee (see p. 54) to people from all walks of life (Luke 7:18–23).
- Jesus brought understanding for the heart and healing for the soul (Luke 10:38–43; John 3–4).
- He helped people find forgiveness (Mark 2:1–12).
- He cast out demons (Luke 4:31–37).
- He freed people from the destructive power of sin. He condemned sin and at the same time showed love to the sinner (John 8:1–11).

Many times we make the same mistake the people of Nazareth made. We think we're God's favorites. Maybe we're favorites because we're from North America or because we're richer than others or because we're biologically related to the people who began the Mennonite Church. None of those qualities make us better or God's favorites. God doesn't have favorites. God loves all people equally.

Voice A: "Gentle Jesus, meek and mild?" Does that song really describe Jesus? He stood up to people. He healed people on the Sabbath and the Pharisees opposed him and he got angry at them.

Voice B: If you're talking about the story in Mark 3:1–6, then the Bible says he "looked around at them with anger; he was grieved at their hardness of heart" (verse 5).

Voice A: Okay, I get the combo of anger and grief. But he was still angry. He had feelings. He was brave enough to stand up to people. He knew when to be gentle and when to let them have it.

Like God at the time of the exodus, Jesus saw oppression of all kinds and he delivered people from that oppression.

Love for the enemy. One such person who needed to be set free was a young lawyer, who asks Jesus what he must do to inherit eternal life. Jesus recites for him the great commandment from the Law: "You shall love the Lord your God with all your heart and with all your soul and with all your strength and with all your mind and your neighbor as yourself. . . . Do this, and you will live" (Luke 10:25–28; see also Deuteronomy 6:4–5 and Leviticus 19:18). But wanting to justify himself, the lawyer asks, "Well, who is my neighbor?"

So, Jesus tells a parable. Three people see a wounded man lying on the road. The first and second ones are religious men, a priest and a Levite. They don't stop to help the dying man, probably so they won't defile themselves and ruin their chances to do religious duties at the temple. But a careful reading of the Bible story says that these two were going "down" from Jerusalem to Jericho, so they had already done their temple duties! A third man also comes by—a Samaritan. He stops and helps the wounded man, even going so far as to pay for him to have special care at an inn (Luke 10:25–37).

The story looks innocent enough until we realize that Samaritans were despised people, looked down on by many because of their mixed ancestry. But it is the unacceptable Samaritan who is the obvious hero of Jesus' story, the one who truly loves his neighbor. Jesus wants the young lawyer to see that godliness is more than obeying God's rules and regulations. He wants to free the lawyer from the oppression of his own prejudice. He wants him to be able to see God, even in those whom society rejects.

Forgiveness for all. But what happens when the lawyer—or we as Christians—can't meet such high standards? In another parable,

---

Voice A: There are a lot of stories in the Gospels where Jesus speaks a word and evil spirits come out of people. So, did Jesus really cast out demons? What does that even mean? Does this kind of deliverance still happen today?

Michele: It does, yes. Some people emphasize the presence of evil in larger systems rather than individual demonic possession. By this I mean institutions, even religious ones, that attempt to have the highest authority, to become God themselves. The apostle Paul calls these institutions the "cosmic powers of this present darkness" (Ephesians 6:12). Other believers today might see evil bothering us primarily through demons or evil spirits (Ephesians 6:11). Jesus cast out demons (Mark 1:21–28; 5:1–20), and he challenged the powers (Mark 2:1–12). So, I think the question of evil spirts in our present day is both a spiritual and a systemic matter.

Jesus tells of two sons: the young one who runs off with his share of the inheritance and the older one who stays home as he should. After burning through his money on riotous living, the younger son faces starvation. Coming to his senses, he decides to return home to beg forgiveness and at least try to work for his father. All this time, the father has been watching for him, longing for him, loving the profligate younger son just as much as he loves the steadfast older son. So when the younger boy gets within sight, the father runs out to greet him, forgiving him before the words "I'm sorry" can tumble out of his mouth (Luke 15:11–32).

We are all like the boy who ran off. We sin, we screw up, we are unable to love the despised Samaritans in our town. And God watches out the window every day, looking for us. When we start to come home, God races out and embraces us with love.

Voice A: Okay, but what about the older son? Finish the story.

Voice B: He got mad when the father threw a huge "welcome home" party for his undeserving brother.

Voice C: I can see why he'd be mad if he had never gotten a party.

Voice A: Who said he never got a party? Maybe he just didn't go to the parties that were meant for him all along.

Voice C: It's hard for people to be happy when others get what they need instead of the bad punishment they deserve.

Voice B: Or in other words, mercy.

Voice C: Yes. But we all sin. And we all need the love of Jesus, shown so clearly in his life and death. We are all the younger son.

Good news: living from the heart

Jesus brought good news for everyone. This is made especially clear in the Sermon on the Mount (Matthew 5–7). In many ways, this collection of teachings mirrors the high ideals that God gave the Israelites in the wilderness. Jesus calls his followers to love their enemies (5:43–48), pray with true motives (6:5–15), and give up worrying over what they will eat or wear (6:25–34).

Religious leaders made many extra rules to ensure that, at least on the outside, they were obeying God's laws. Jesus cut to the heart of the matter. Jesus addressed attitudes. Those who refrain from murder but still harbor hate in their hearts are as bad as murderers (5:21–26). Those who have lust in their hearts are as bad as those who commit adultery (5:27–30). In one powerful hyperbole, Jesus suggests that people cut off their hands and gouge out their eyes if doing so will help them change their ways (5:29–30). People need a change of heart, and that goes even deeper than changing or losing our limbs! Jesus was trying to get at the root of ethical choices, which literally is what the word *radical* suggests.

Going beyond words and actions. What does it mean to follow Jesus? What is involved in being a Christian? Jesus said a lot of things that can be hard to figure out. In John 3, he tells Nicodemus he has to be "born again" (see John 3:1–8). A rich young ruler asks Jesus, "What must I do to inherit eternal life?" Jesus tells him to sell all his possessions and give the money to the poor (Luke 18:18–30). According to the Sermon on the Mount, one becomes a child of God by loving one's enemies (Matthew 5:44–45). Other times Jesus simply tells people, "Follow me" (Mark 1:17).

The early church expressed salvation somewhat differently. In Acts 2:38, the apostle Peter urges the crowd to "Repent and be baptized every one of you in the name of Jesus Christ so that your sins may be forgiven, and you will receive the gift of the Holy Spirit." Paul writes in Romans 10:9 that if you "confess with your mouth that Jesus is Lord and believe in your heart that God raised him from the dead, you will be saved." How do you understand all these things put together?

Perhaps the Sermon on the Mount can help us understand. In Matthew 7:21, Jesus says, "Not everyone who says to me, 'Lord, Lord,' will enter the kingdom of heaven, but only the one who does the will of my Father in heaven." At first glance, this statement cautions us against just saying the right words or simply agreeing to a set of statements. Our faith must be deeper than that.

It must also go deeper than actions. Jesus continues, "On that day many will say to me, 'Lord, Lord, did we not prophesy in your

Voice A: I don't appreciate the whole "turning the other cheek" idea (Matthew 5:38–42). Doing so would make us doormats.

Voice B: If you understand Jesus' culture, that's not true. To turn the other cheek was a way for a peasant to tell a soldier, "I'm your equal."

Michele: That's correct. So, Jesus is urging us to resist evil, which means we don't have to be doormats, and yet, it's nonviolent resistance. And creative.

The Sermon on the Mount sounds like an impossible standard to live by.

Yet nothing is impossible with God.

The Beatitudes

Jesus' Sermon on the Mount (Matthew 5–7) is one of the most quoted summaries of Jesus' radical teaching about how one lives under God's reign. It begins with a statement about what makes people truly happy in life:

Blessed are the poor in spirit, for theirs is the kingdom of heaven.

Blessed are those who mourn, for they will be comforted.

Blessed are the meek, for they will inherit the earth.

Blessed are those who hunger and thirst for righteousness, for they will be filled.

Blessed are the merciful, for they will receive mercy.

Blessed are the pure in heart, for they will see God.

Blessed are the peacemakers, for they will be called children of God.

Blessed are those who are persecuted for the sake of righteousness, for theirs is the kingdom of heaven.

Blessed are you when people revile you and persecute you and utter all kinds of evil against you falsely on my account. Rejoice and be glad, for your reward is great in heaven, for in the same way they persecuted the prophets who were before you.

—Matthew 5:3–12

Different ways to say "I'm a Christian":

- I'm a believer in Jesus.
- I'm a follower of Christ.
- I have a relationship with Jesus.
- I'm born again.
- I'm saved.
- I have surrendered my life to Christ.
- I have accepted Jesus as my Savior and Lord.

On the one hand, it's not a big deal how you identify yourself as a Christian. These are different ways of saying the same thing. On the other hand, each expression has a certain emphasis. If you stress that you're a *follower* of Jesus, you might start to emphasize outer obedience to God more than the grace and spiritual transformation that are part of being a Christian. If you stress that you are *saved*, you might begin to think Christianity is only about a conversion event that secures you a place in heaven someday. Being a Christian involves an event *and* a process. God reaches out to us and we respond—and keep responding in a relationship that grows every day. Being a Christian is simple, yet it's a mystery.

name, and cast out demons in your name, and do many mighty works in your name?' Then I will declare to them, 'I never knew you; go away from me, you who behave lawlessly" (Matthew 7:22–23). Not only does our salvation need to be deeper than saying the right words, it also has to be more than outward actions, even spectacular acts of faith.

Both words and actions can fake the real thing. But what is the real thing? Salvation is rich enough and mysterious enough that people use different ways to explain it. But real salvation always means a change in us. Like Nicodemus, we are born again. We act differently because we have experienced an inner change. Part of salvation is asking God to forgive us our sins and to heal the relationship with God that sin has destroyed. We also allow God to transform us so that *all* our relationships are restored. We confess that Jesus is our Lord not because saying those words will save us, but because we serve a different savior than the rest of the world does. We live lives that please God not because we have to in order to become or remain Christians, but because that's who we are. We have a new identity in Christ.

Making it personal. The disciples are mystified over who their rabbi is. Like their fellow Jews, they're expecting a different type of messiah. Why doesn't Jesus get rid of the Romans by force? Why doesn't he let people proclaim him as Messiah, especially after one of his miraculous healings? And why does he count sex workers, Roman soldiers, tax collectors, and Samaritans among his friends? To add to the confusion, Jesus talks about his own upcoming suffering and death.

Jesus knows about their confusion. So one day he asks them, "Who do people say that the Son of Man is?" They answer, "Some

What do people today need to be saved from spiritually, physically, and emotionally? I believe Jesus longs to heal us from the bondage of our sin and also from things like anxiety, depression, loneliness, and hunger. If Jesus was with us in human form today, how would he meet people's deepest needs? And perhaps an even more important question: how well is the church meeting people's needs today?

say John the Baptist but others Elijah and still others Jeremiah or one of the prophets." Then he asks them, "But who do you say that I am?" Simon Peter replies confidently, "You are the Messiah, the Son of the living God." Jesus is pleased with his answer and says, "You are Peter [literally meaning Rock], and on this rock I will build my church, and the gates of Hades will not prevail against it" (Matthew 16:13–18).

Voice A: So, is Peter the rock the church is built on?

Michele: I think the rock Jesus refers to is Peter's confession that Jesus is Lord.

Jesus then tells them what it means for him to be the Messiah (Matthew 16:21–28). This is the hardest thing for the disciples to understand. It means refusing to compromise one's obedience to God. It means saying no to violence and yes to suffering love. For Jesus, it means death. For many of the disciples, it will mean their deaths as well.

By our lives, every day, we say to the world who we think Jesus is.

Who do you say Jesus is? Who does your life say Jesus is?

Peter is so shocked at Jesus' words that he scolds him. How can the Messiah allow himself to suffer and die? And what does Jesus mean by rising again in three days? Jesus' temptation in the wilderness has snuck back in: Peter is suggesting that he avoid the cross. But in Matthew 16:23 Jesus retorts, "Get behind me, Satan!"

Salvation: a done deal, or something in process?

Voice A: If salvation means all of our relationships are restored, I'm in trouble, because I can't say that about my relationships.

Michele: I see your point. We are saved *in* our brokenness as much as we are saved *out* of our brokenness.

Voice A: Wait, if some of my relationships with people are not in good standing, then I'm still okay?

Michele: This reality is another paradox. We experience salvation when we say yes to Jesus (Ephesians 2:8), but we also "work out" that salvation in our lives (1 Corinthians 1:18; Philippians 2:12).

We also look forward to the day when our salvation will be complete (Romans 8:18–23). When we don't feel like loving our enemies or feeding the hungry, it doesn't mean we're not Christians anymore. It means that God is still in process with us.

Voice A: What about the necessity of violence to liberate oppressed people? Sure, in a perfect world, we can offer nonviolent protest and advocate our way into better systems. But the people who benefit from the injustice will defend their harmful actions with their last breaths. We live in an evil world, and I think that sometimes we have to use violence to dismantle the evil systems.

Michele: Great question and concerns. But let's take the long view of justice, to borrow from Martin Luther King Jr. Nonviolence isn't just about not killing people, it's about resisting even the little oppressive acts that happen day in and day out. One of the positive hallmarks of Anabaptist Christians is their combined pursuit of peace and justice. Jesus did this as well. He didn't just say to love your enemies. He slammed the religious leaders for their oppressive ways and wanted them to be held accountable.

Voice A: So we have to stop all the little injustices before they build up to war.

Michele: That's right. It takes a long time to create a just society, and we have to work toward it every single day. The end never justifies the means, which is admittedly easier said than done when you're being oppressed.

What about us? As we reflect on who Jesus is and hear the good news of Jesus and see the evidence of his love, we have to respond in some way. It's not enough to know about Jesus and salvation. It's not enough to be able to explain what everything means in the story and how it all fits together. Considering this knowledge, you must make a choice. Will you follow Jesus? Will you accept God's great love for you, trusting in this love and letting that transform your life? Will you say yes to him? Will you let Jesus change every aspect of your life beginning now, with the promise of a continued, loving and growing relationship?

What does it mean to "follow" Jesus? What differences and similarities are there between the way the twelve disciples followed Jesus and the way we follow him today?

Summing it up

From the beginning, God communicated with humans through the Law and prophets, through the written stories of God's dealings with the Israelites, and through direct encounters with people. The Story was powerful, but the people got the message all twisted around. They interpreted God's message to fit their own desires. Through Jesus, God took on human form and lived among us, experiencing with us the pains, frustrations, and joys of being human. (He died and he rose again, but we will explore this in the next chapter.) In doing so, Jesus showed us the true nature and will of God. Through Jesus, we have a glimpse of God (John 1:1–14, 18; Hebrews 1:1–3). What wonderful news!

People interpreted God's message to fit their own needs. To what extent are we doing the same thing?

- *Jesus is fully God and fully human.* We take by faith that Jesus is one hundred percent God and one hundred percent human. If we overemphasize the humanity of Jesus, we take his ethics seriously but can only see him as a good moral teacher. If we overemphasize the divinity of Christ, we get excited about what Christ can do for us spiritually, but we tend to ignore his teachings about what is right and wrong.
- *Jesus chose to be a servant.* Jesus made a deliberate choice to be the kind of messiah who would not use military force. Instead, he would defeat evil through obedient love for God. This was—and is—the highest and most powerful form of power. We are called to make that same choice today.
- *Through Jesus, God offered spiritual and physical salvation to everyone.* Jesus brought freedom from oppression of all kinds—physical, social, and spiritual. To emphasize one kind of deliverance over others distorts the true meaning of salvation.
- *Jesus calls people to follow him.* Jesus didn't only heal people and teach the crowds. He gathered a group of disciples and trained them to continue his work in the world. We, too, are called into a journey with Jesus.

A spiritual discipline to practice

Reread the story of the prodigal son, found in Luke 15:11–32. Place yourself in the shoes of the younger son and imagine that God, like the loving father, wants to write you a love letter. Write down what you hear inside you.

Now place yourself in the shoes of the older son and imagine that God, like the loving father, wants to write you a love letter. Write down what you hear inside.

TOPICS IN CHAPTER 5

- Jesus: a threat to the powers that be
- Jesus' love, service, sacrifice
- Why Jesus died
- What Jesus' death has to do with us
- Why Jesus rose again
- Why the resurrection matters

STORYLINE

- The Last Supper
- Jesus washes the disciples' feet
- Jesus' trial and crucifixion
- Jesus' resurrection

5. Mission Accomplished

IN SOME WAYS, THINGS LOOKED THE SAME when Jesus finished his work in Galilee and "set his face" toward Jerusalem (Luke 9:53). He still healed the sick and he still taught the people with an authority they had never before encountered, but now Jesus seems more determined. There is a look in his eyes. He talks about rejection and suffering (Luke 9:21–22). He tells the disciples that they too must bear their crosses, they too must be willing to suffer for the sake of God and others (9:23–26). Even though foxes have holes to sleep in and birds have nests to rest in, Jesus says that the Son of Man has nowhere to lay his head (9:57–62). He talks about his own upcoming death.

Confrontation: Jesus' last hours

Triumphal entry. All this suffering and death talk was hard for his followers to comprehend on the day Jesus rode into Jerusalem. The crowds loved him. It was Passover, the sacred festival that celebrated the time God liberated the Israelites from slavery in Egypt. Pilgrims traveled far to attend this festival and eat a special meal that reenacted the last meal the slaves ate before they were rescued out of Egypt. The streets were full. Passover always raised the Jews' hopes that maybe this year the Messiah would come. In the past, God acted in a dramatic way to free them from slavery. Many understood prophets like Isaiah to say that in the future someone new would come who would deliver them again—the Messiah.[7] As Jesus' procession nears the city, the people shout "Hosanna!" (meaning "Lord, save!") and put their cloaks and palm branches on the ground to form a carpet for the donkey to walk on (Luke 19:28–40). Is this the one who will free them from the Romans?

Temple confrontation. As much as the common folk love Jesus, however, the religious leaders fear and hate him. What Jesus does at the temple that next day only confirms those fears. Jesus sees moneychangers and merchants doing business in the temple—and he is infuriated. Not only were they most likely overcharging folks, but this noisy marketplace is set up in the very spot reserved for non-Jews to pray and worship. In his anger, Jesus overturns the tables and sets the livestock free. The merchants and moneychangers run in every direction. Jesus scolds, "My house shall be called a house of prayer for all the nations. But you have made it a den of robbers" (see Mark 11:15–17; see also John 2:13–22).

Voice A: What was behind Jesus' action in the temple (Mark 11:15–17)? Does this story justify the use of violence to defeat evil? Why or why not?

Michele: Some maybe would say it does, but I don't think so. Using the example of flipping over tables and driving out animals as justification for war or violence is a significant stretch.

The temple leaders are furious. Jesus' ministry is already a threat to their way of life. He heals on the Sabbath. He talks with Gentiles, Samaritans, and sex workers. He tells the crowds that their righteousness must go beyond the righteousness of the religious leaders, the scribes, and Pharisees. And the common people hang on his every word. Now the riot in the temple is more than these leaders can tolerate, so they accelerate their plans to get rid of him (Luke 22:1–2).

See the Confession of Faith summary of Article 12 about communion on page 184.

The Last Supper. That Thursday, Jesus gathers with his disciples to celebrate the Passover meal. At Passover each Jewish family reenacted the night when God liberated those enslaved in Egypt (see pp. 46–50). In the original Passover, the Israelites were instructed

Jesus as Lamb

Voice A: Okay, this is getting back to the exodus as a picture of our salvation, right? The perfect lamb is like Jesus. All the enslaved people had to do was put the blood over their door and the death angel would pass over them.

Voice B: And crossing the Red Sea is like baptism. The Promised Land is like heaven.

Michele: This is one picture of salvation and there are others. When Jesus and his friends shared the Passover meal, Jesus gave the traditional elements, bread and wine, a new meaning. He broke the bread and said, "Take and eat. This is my body." He took the cup of wine and said, "Drink, this is my blood." Jesus was honoring the old covenant that God made with the Israelites, and at the same time he was initiating a new covenant. He was thinking ahead to the shedding of his own blood (Luke 22:14–23).

(See pp. 100, 175, 176 for more on Jesus as the "lamb who was slain" and p. 58 for more on covenants.)

The Lord's Supper (Communion)

The Lord's Supper can help us understand and experience several important things about Jesus and the church. Here are some of those ways:

- We take the Lord's Supper to remember the death of Jesus.
- It helps us look forward to the big banquet of God's kingdom in the future.
- Taking the Lord's Supper also builds unity and care in local groups of believers. The apostle Paul told the Corinthian believers that if they didn't love and care for each other they would totally miss the meaning of the Lord's Supper. They would eat and drink in ways that dishonored Christ (see 1 Corinthians 11:17–34).

So in one way, the Lord's Supper is about the mysterious presence of Jesus right there with you. But in another way, Christ's presence among us depends on something as ordinary as caring for each other as a church.

to prepare lamb and herbs and smear the blood of an unblemished lamb on the doorposts. They ate standing up, ready to leave Egypt at a moment's notice. It was a tense night. The angel of death passed over every house that had the lamb's blood on the door. Where there was no blood on the door, the eldest son was killed (Exodus 12:29–32, 43–49).

Footwashing. If the minds of the disciples aren't boggled yet, they will be soon. Their mouths hang open as their beloved Teacher puts on a servant's apron and kneels down with a basin of water right before their eyes. *Surely not,* they think, *surely Jesus will not wash their feet; that is servants' work!* Yet as he takes the first dust-caked foot in his hands, the disciples know that yes, this is what he means to do. Peter cringes at the idea. "You shall never wash my feet!" Jesus smiles a weary smile. He knows that before Peter—or any of them, for that matter—can be the humble servant leaders they have been called to be, they must first receive that same gentle love (John 13:1–20).

How does the story of the Last Supper and Jesus washing his disciples' feet connect with the meaning of Jesus' death and resurrection?

Betrayal. Jesus startles his friends yet again by announcing that one of them will betray him. All are in shock—except Judas, who had already struck a deal with the enemies of Jesus to turn him over. Judas may have gotten the wrong idea when Jesus cleared out the temple. Maybe he thought that now, especially if forced into the situation, Jesus would fight the Romans with his supernatural power. Perhaps Judas thought he could be the one to give Jesus the incentive he needed. In any case, Jesus urges Judas, "Do quickly what you are going to do" (John 13:27). And Judas walks out the door to find the religious leaders.

See the Confession of Faith summary of Article 13 about foot-washing on page 184.

Michele: Some Christian groups, including many Mennonites, practice a ceremony of footwashing, often during the same service as communion. In pairs, people take turns kneeling down to wash each other's feet in a basin as Jesus instructed his disciples to do (John 13:14). What do you think of that practice?

Voice A: It's not been my experience much to wash feet, so I'm pretty uncomfortable with it.

Michele: That makes sense. It's not like performing this, or any other ritual for that matter, brings you salvation. When I do wash feet, I feel queasy at the time too. Yet when I choose to wash feet in spite of my discomfort, something happens to me. It helps break me open to love the person whose feet I am washing. Washing feet means being a servant to everyone you meet—every day. This is especially true of people you have a hard time loving. Being a servant is not just doing nice things for others. It's living in such a way that you really do care about them; you serve them for their sakes, not yours.

It even means letting others serve you.

The rest of the group trudges to the Garden of Gethsemane. Realizing what lies ahead, Jesus needs time to pray. He is in agony. Being fully human, he dreads the pain of torture and death and shrinks from the coming humiliation. And so, in this late hour, he asks God to take away this "cup" of suffering if possible (Mark 14:32–36). The temptations from the wilderness loom once again in front of him. He must have wondered, *Is there any other way?*

Yet he knew the answer. The only way to avoid suffering was to take matters into his own hands, to somehow force the people to follow him through military might, economic incentives, or through a never-ending parade of miracles. To proceed any other way than faithful obedience to God would be to compromise that obedience. Yet to obey, he knew, would be to die. "Not what I want but what you want," (Matthew 26:39; Mark 14:36) he finally prays, fully committing himself to God.

Arrest. Jesus' decision comes none too soon, for Judas is already in the garden, leading the temple guards and soldiers to arrest him. Peter pulls a sword and takes a swing at the nearest enemy, cutting off the ear of one of the servants. Surely, thinks Peter, if there ever was an appropriate time for violence, if there ever was a time when the ends justified the means, surely it is now when his leader is in danger. But Jesus says no. If he needs protection, he explains, he can call thousands of angels for help. "All who take the sword will die by the sword," Jesus says (Matthew 26:52). Jesus then heals the ear of his enemy (Luke 22:51).

Trial. After a long night of interrogation in a trial that made mockery of justice, Jesus stands before the Roman governor, Pilate. Pilate knows an innocent man when he sees one. He tries several times to set Jesus free. But Pilate himself is pinned in a

The four Gospels in the New Testament—Matthew, Mark, Luke, and John—each tell the story of Jesus in a slightly different way. Especially in the closing chapters, we see each gospel writer emphasizing different details of the story. John, for example, does not tell about the Last Supper, but he does tell about Jesus washing the disciples' feet. In the account of the resurrection, Matthew describes an angel greeting the women at the tomb; Luke describes two men in dazzling white clothes; Mark recounts a young man at the tomb; and John doesn't mention angels but says Jesus appears to Mary.

For a rewarding Bible study challenge, compare the closing chapters of the Gospels to discover what each author may have wanted to emphasize. For our discussion here, we draw on details from all four stories, as you can see from the references in parentheses. At the same time, we recognize that trying to build a composite story should not diminish each story's merits.

corner, for the religious leaders are blackmailing him. "If you release this man, you are no friend of the emperor," they said. "We have no king but the emperor" (see John 19:12–15). Jesus' enemies wanted to get rid of Jesus so much that they were willing to compromise one of their most precious beliefs: the sovereignty of their own nation under God. In times past, the Jews risked death rather than pay allegiance to foreign rulers. Now these scribes and Pharisees hail Caesar as their king, because Jesus is that much of a threat.

Is Jesus perceived as a threat by people today? Or is the Jesus people see, through us, just a drummed up version of what we want him to be?

Our cosmic butler, giving us whatever we want to make our lives easier.

A God who will justify our violence.

A homeboy Jesus who makes us feel good and have happy lives.

It's not that Jesus doesn't want us to have happy lives, but knowing him really is more than that. If Jesus were only permissive and positive today, nobody would kill him at all. So, what does it mean if Jesus isn't perceived as a threat today? Are we manufacturing a Jesus in our own image?

Crucifixion. Pilate sentences Jesus to be crucified, along with two others. It is a horrible ordeal. Jesus has already suffered from flogging, all night interrogations, and the emotional distress of knowing what lay ahead. Now, he will be put on a wooden cross, where his hands and feet will literally be nailed to the wood. Then, tearing his flesh even more, the whole cross will be hoisted into the ground. Jesus will hang, literally, with the weight of his own body causing immense pain with every breath.

Crucifixion was not only horribly painful, but also a public display of humiliation. The people come and mock Jesus. "He saved others; let him save himself if he is the Messiah" (Luke 23:35). If they only knew! By not saving himself, he is saving them.

Although the pain is almost unbearable, Jesus stays conscious enough to speak and to take some control of this situation. He asks God to forgive the ones who crucified him (Luke 23:34). He offers forgiveness and comfort to the repentant man being crucified next to him (Luke 23:39–43). He cares for his mother in the midst of his own pain (John 19:26). Darkness falls over the area for three hours as Jesus wrestles with pain and the feeling of God's abandonment. Then with a loud cry, Jesus gives himself into God's care and dies (Luke

23:46). A Roman centurion offers a final testimony after Jesus dies. He says, "Surely this man was the Son of God" (Mark 15:39 NIV).

Why Jesus had to die

Why did Jesus have to die? This has been an important question through the ages. How we answer that question helps determine how we understand God, our own relationship with God, and what it means to be a Christian. How we answer this question helps determine our behavior.

First, we have to remember why Jesus came to earth in the first place. It's inadequate to think he only came to earth to die. If he only came to be a sacrifice for our sin, then we could ignore his life and teachings. But Jesus also came to live and show us who God really is. Jesus so threatened the powers who were in control (see the discussion on the powers on pp. 37, 83) that those in authority killed him. And when he refused to budge from what he knew was the right thing to do and refused to use violence, even when authorities threatened him with death, he defeated the evil that put him to death. We are to be like Jesus. We need to be willing to do the right thing even if it means being persecuted or killed.

In simple language, we can say that Jesus loved you and me enough to come to earth to live and die, and because he did, we can know and love God. The Bible says this in several different and more complex ways, some of which are outlined below. None of these ways of explaining why Jesus died should be taken by itself. Some of these views can be easily misunderstood. But together they all help us understand this important concept.

1. Jesus' life and death are perfect examples of sacrificial, suffering love. Through his life, teaching, and death, Jesus showed us how to respond to evil—through nonviolence and enemy love. When we see the suffering and death of an innocent Jesus, we are morally revolted and take a hard look at our own violence and sin. We are called to experience God's salvation by reflecting similar sacrificial love in our own lives as disciples (1 Peter 2:21).

There is a weakness in this view. It's great to have the perfect example to follow. But is it enough? Is it enough to just reflect on the life of Jesus and then imitate that life? Or do we need a power greater than we are to truly conquer evil in a nonviolent way?

2. Jesus, through his death, paid for our sins. Another way to think about why Jesus was killed is that Jesus died to pay for our sins (Romans 4:25). The metaphor goes like this: our sins rack up a debt that we can't pay. It's like being a servant who lives on the master's land without being able to pay his bills. A variation on this theme is that we've committed a crime and the punishment is death (Romans 6:23). It's like being a criminal standing before the judge. In both metaphors, Jesus comes and pays the price or takes the punishment for us. In the Old Testament times, the people "atoned" for their sins by sacrificing pure lambs. In a sense, the animals took the punishment for sin, rather than the people. Jesus is called the Lamb of God because he took punishment intended for sinners (John 1:29).

Some misunderstand this view when they believe that God is an angry god or a God who demands payment. It's true that the priests in the Old Testament sacrificed animals, but it's likely that they didn't do it so much to cool down God's anger as it was to show the people the terrible consequences of sin.

Another weakness of this view is that it portrays God as a God who demands someone's death (Jesus') in order to satisfy God's honor or justice. What kind of a God is that? John 3:16 says that God sent Jesus because God loves the whole world, not because God is angry and needs Jesus to take the heat for our wrongs. God doesn't need a payment so he can forgive us. Jesus forgave a man's sins in Mark 2:1–12 and he hadn't even died on the cross yet.

A final weakness of this view on its own is that it makes salvation from sin a purely spiritual matter that takes place outside of history and through an invisible transaction between God and Jesus. God's heart is changed by Jesus' death, not ours. In this limited understanding, our salvation has nothing to do with how we live our lives. This kind of "salvation" isn't concerned with the broken relationships we may have with others or the hold that sin or real-life oppression has in our lives.

3. Christ is the victor. In this view, Jesus is in a cosmic battle where he defeats the powers of the devil, evil, and death through a life lived in total, faithful obedience. When Jesus chooses to confront evil and also chooses to be nonviolent, he knows it will mean his death. Ironically, it is in his death—when he looks the most helpless—that he defeats evil. How? When threatened and made to suffer horribly, Jesus does not retaliate. This exposes evil for what it really is, thus breaking its power. Then God raises Jesus from death, proving that Jesus did the right thing. It also secures the victory that he, and all of us, can have over death (Colossians 2:15). We, too, have this resurrection power. Jesus' resurrection shows that there is a power greater than evil. In many ways, this view includes the helpful parts of the other metaphors but transforms them. Humans are changed rather than an angry God needing to be changed. We are set free.

Here's yet another way to look at it. Jesus saved us not only by his death but also by his life, his teachings, his resurrection, and the coming of the Spirit. In all these ways, Jesus worked to heal one or more of the four broken relationships that sin destroys. Sin breaks our relationship with God. Jesus healed that relationship by offering forgiveness during his life and through the cross and also by showing us the incredible loving character of God! Sin breaks the relationship between us and other humans, and Jesus heals that relationship when he demonstrates eating with marginalized people (Matthew 9:9–11), by his teachings about enemy love (Matthew 5:43–48), and by giving us the Spirit, who can help us do what seems impossible—that is, love our enemies. Finally, sin breaks the relationship between us and our inner selves. Over and over Jesus took away people's shame by healing their bodies and forgiving their sins (Mark 2:1–12) and loving them so they could love themselves. Jesus still does that today. And the broken relationship we have with the physical world? Jesus takes care of that with his resurrection and also with his loving attention to the physical needs of people.

It's not that the cross isn't important to our salvation. It really is! But sometimes, when we fail to look at all of Jesus' life, we may think only about the cross as payment for our sins, and then we settle for a salvation that only heals our broken relationship with God. That relationship is an important one. But Jesus wants to provide a salvation for us that is more than a ticket to heaven. Jesus wants to forgive us, and also to restore us and transform us into the persons who we were always meant to be. Jesus wants to heal every part of us, and he wants to heal the broken evil systems in this world.

The meaning of Jesus' death is complex. It's important to remember that Jesus' life, teachings, miracles, death, and resurrection all work together to heal the four broken relationships. It's also important to see that God's impulse toward us is love. The cross, as well as the rest of Jesus' life, all point to a love that is beyond description. The cross shows that God will go to all lengths to love us. Nothing, not even the threat of death, can stop this love. We can rest in that promise.

atonement: *how we become "at one" with God. At-one-ment.*

Burial. According to Jewish custom, dead bodies were to be removed from public view. With the Sabbath beginning the evening Jesus died, a secret follower of Jesus named Joseph of Arimathea moved quickly to honor the law. He asks permission to bury Jesus' body in a tomb he owns, and the authorities grant his request (Mark 15:42–47). As for Jesus' followers, most of whom had abandoned Jesus during his trial and crucifixion, the Sabbath itself was a sad day. They hid in fear behind locked doors.

Resurrection. The events of early Sunday morning are told selectively in each of the gospel accounts (Matthew 28:1–10; Mark 16:1–8; Luke 24:1–12; John 20:1–18). Early Sunday morning several

Voice A: All of these things are important, I know, but you know what really hits me? Jesus loves me. Jesus loves me. That's what it's all about for me.

Voice B: I am a sinner; I was caught in a mess of sin, and Jesus brought me out. That's what I'm thankful for.

Voice C: I think it's hard for some people to really believe God loves them. They have messed up so much, and I don't know, maybe salvation for them is just someone coming in and helping them get out of the mess.

Michele: But salvation is important for people whose lives aren't in a mess, too. You know, I wasn't in a big mess when I wanted to begin a relationship with Jesus. Guilt was kind of pushed on me, more than what I felt myself. I knew I was supposed to feel bad about my life. I can feel guilty about not feeling guilty, you know? But for me, I wanted to know something, Someone. I just wanted to know God.

Voice A: If Jesus died only as the perfect lamb who paid for our sins, then we can be thankful for that, but we don't have to be exactly like Jesus.

Voice B: Right, because none of us are perfect and so none of us could ever be that perfect lamb.

Voice A: But Jesus told us that we, too, are to deny ourselves and take up our cross and follow him (Luke 9:23). So where does that leave us?

Michele: Good point.

Voice A: And when we challenge injustice and also commit to being nonviolent, we know that evil will strike back at us.

Michele: Yes. And that is how we carry our own cross.

Voice A: Didn't God need to use violence—ultimately—in order to save us? I mean, if the only way we can have our sins be forgiven is for Jesus to pay for our sins with his blood, then God needs someone to be killed, and that's violence. So, violence must be good, or at least okay in some circumstances.

Michele: That's true only if you see one reason for Jesus' death on the cross: payment for sin. Remember that the Bible uses several metaphors to describe why Jesus died. Payment for sin is only one of them—and a shaky one at that.

Voice A: Didn't Jesus forgive sins before he died? Like when he forgave and healed the paralyzed man in Mark 2.

Michele: Yes, he did. But if we accept the idea that Jesus was also killed on the cross because he both challenged evil and chose nonviolence, then his death has more than one meaning.

Voice A: And it demonstrates how to live our lives—by also fighting evil nonviolently.

Michele: I think we also need to wonder if in truth whether the metaphor of God needing to have a blood payment is compatible with what we know about God. Maybe the cross is an act of ultimate love that goes all the way. Humans could do the worst thing possible—kill God's son—and still God will love them.

women followers of Jesus set out early to finish the job of embalming Jesus' body. Grief filled their hearts, and worry, too. How would they move the heavy stone placed over the tomb? The Jewish leaders had requested the stone and guards to make sure no one stole the body. It would be impossible for these women to move it by themselves.

But . . . what? The stone was rolled away! They couldn't believe their eyes! Did someone steal the body after all? They peek inside. The body is gone. Something terrible has happened. Someone took the body! Still in shock, they turn to see a bright light and . . . an angel? Jesus has risen from the dead, the angel says.

Going as fast as they can, the women run to tell the others. The men are in shock and disbelief. As John tells it, Peter and John run to see for themselves that the tomb is empty (John 20:3). The graveclothes lay by themselves. Perhaps? Can it be true? Is Jesus alive? It is too wonderful to be true!

Later, as Mary Magdalene lingers by the tomb, she meets a man. At first, she thinks it is the gardener. But as he greets her by name, she realizes it is Jesus. She kneels at his feet in worship. At Jesus' bidding, Mary runs to tell the other disciples that she has seen the Lord.

In the next days and weeks, Jesus appears in various places and times to the disciples and others. In some ways, the body of Jesus is like their own bodies. He eats with them (Luke 24:42; John 21:9–14). He has the scars of crucifixion on his hands, feet, and side (Luke 24:39–40). In other ways, Jesus has a different kind of body. He can appear and disappear. He walks through locked doors (Luke 24:31, 36). Not only does the Spirit of Jesus interact with people, but the same body walks among the disciples, complete with the holes in his wrists and feet. His crucified body is different, and yet the same.

Ascension. After forty days, Jesus and his disciples are all together. The disciples ask Jesus if he will now restore the kingdom to Israel (Acts 1:6). With this question, they're urging Jesus to establish God's reign through the nation of Israel. They still don't understand that Jesus is ushering in a kingdom of all people groups, a kingdom that people choose to be a part of. God's reign truly had begun—not in the way of a nation-state or government, but a kingdom of God's values that can thrive in any government. Jesus redirects the disciples. He tells them that they will receive power from the Holy Spirit that will help them be witnesses to this kingdom, starting in Jerusalem and going to every part of the world. Then Jesus ascends into heaven. He's lifted up and a cloud takes him away. Two men in bright white appear to those watching below. They tell the disciples that Jesus will return some day in the same way they had just seen him leave.

Why Jesus' resurrection is so important

The resurrection was a central part of the story as Jesus' followers told it (see Acts 2:29–36). It established that Jesus was indeed God's Son and the Messiah—Lord over all things, including the power of death. In his letter to the Corinthians, Paul writes that if Jesus didn't rise from the dead, their faith was useless (1 Corinthians 15:14). Christ's resurrection is a guarantee of our own resurrection as believers. We can praise God with Paul and say, "Death has been swallowed up in victory. . . . Thanks be to God, who gives us the victory through our Lord Jesus Christ!" (1 Corinthians 15:54–57).

Imagine Christianity without the resurrection of Jesus. Do you think Christian faith would have survived without it?

The resurrection impacts our ethics. There were some people in the Corinthian church who thought that physical things were useless, including our bodies, or at least inferior to the spiritual world (1 Corinthians 6:12–20; 15:35–58). So they reasoned that if their bodies were not going to be a part of their eternal life with God, then they could do anything they wanted with them. They had unlimited sexual partners and drank and ate their bodies into ruin. Paul explained to them that this was against what God had said from the beginning—that creation was good. We are to take care of our bodies in obedience to God and because we know that God can redeem our bodies and make them new. We are also to protect our planet—the land, air, soil, animals, and plants. The resurrection helps us know that God loves the physical world since God raised Jesus back to physical life.

How does Jesus' death and resurrection affect your life today?

The resurrection gives us courage in the face of death. Our confidence in the resurrection also helps us to take risks in following Christ. Paul connects the resurrection in a logical way to his own life as a traveling missionary. Paul could face the possibility of death every day because he knew that if he died, he could look

Jesus calls us to carry our own cross. That could mean standing up to a bully or standing in solidarity with the unpopular person at school. What does that mean for you?

forward to resurrection life with Christ. The resurrection helped give him courage to face the dangers that he had to face as a believer (1 Corinthians 15:30–34; Philippians 1:21–26). The resurrection can also be a source of great strength for us today when we think about the risks and dangers of following Christ faithfully.

Summing it up

- *The life, death, and resurrection of Jesus are at the heart of our faith.* Jesus died for our sins (1 Corinthians 15:3), opening a way for us to receive God's forgiveness and reconciliation. Jesus' death also shows us the power of faith and of God's love in the face of violence and evil. This impacts how we live as Jesus' followers.
- *Jesus showed that, by the way he lived his life, he was a threat to the powers that be.* When we follow Jesus, we too may face opposition from the world. But like Jesus, we look beyond suffering, even death, to our resurrection.
- *Jesus taught and modeled servant leadership.* True leaders, said Jesus, are those who serve. Jesus washed the disciples' feet. He demonstrated a power that is greater than any force on earth: the power of love.
- *Jesus was consistent to the end.* Especially at the time of his crucifixion, Jesus resisted the temptations he had faced in the wilderness. He refused to use force to free himself. He loved his enemies. He was obedient to God to the end. Ironically, when Jesus looked the weakest, hanging on the cross, he was the strongest. Satan, evil, and death were truly defeated through Jesus' obedience to God. The resurrection confirmed that victory.

- *The resurrection proved God's grace and love.* How can humans use their free will to sin horribly and yet see God make all things work out? God stepped into that awesome tension by coming to our world in Jesus. God turned the very worst thing we could do—crucify Jesus—into the thing that defeated evil. We humans can do our worst—murder God—but we cannot destroy God's love for us.

A spiritual discipline to practice

Get together with other Christians and have a footwashing service. Prepare some basins of warm water and have towels and chairs ready. Read John 13:1–17 and then, in pairs, wash each other's feet. It may feel safer to wash the feet of someone of your own gender. When everyone's feet have been washed, you may end the time with a hug. If you don't feel comfortable washing each other's feet, consider washing each other's hands instead.

Atonement

In a narrow view of salvation, we might think that God needs to be changed because God is super angry about our sins. Jesus comes in just the right moment and dies so that God's anger won't squash us to death. But if John 3:16 is right, God sent Jesus because God loved the world, and not because God was super angry.

Now the Bible also says that Jesus' death was a sacrifice. What does that mean?

A sacrifice does not necessarily occur to appease an angry god. If God wanted Jesus' death as a sacrifice, then God is a lot like all the other pagan deities of the ancient world. But the word "sacrifice" can also mean a gift of love, such as people choosing to serve one another sacrificially.

When it comes to understanding atonement, I think you can have a narrow view or a broader view, and this second view is more biblical. In the narrow view, salvation is just about forgiveness. People say the sinner's prayer, they receive forgiveness for their sins, and they are considered to be "saved." And then two weeks later, those same people may be acting just like they did before praying that prayer—they are still just as greedy, as prone to gossip, or likely to be judgmental of their classmates, for example. They are still in bondage to their sins. Why? Because they have accepted a salvation that only heals their relationship to God, as a ticket to heaven.

Instead Jesus' message is: "Don't settle for a secondhand salvation. I want to give you full restoration, full deliverance. I don't just want to forgive you, I want to set you free so you don't keep on sinning." Just like God rescued the slaves out of Egypt because the Lord cared about their physical bondage, Jesus fed the five thousand hungry people on the hillside (Mark 6:30–44). And just like God gave the Israelites the Ten Commandments as the start of their deliverance from sin bondage, so too Jesus both forgave people and offered deliverance from their addictions, like the rich young ruler in Luke 18:18–25. In Luke 8:40–56 Jesus heals a woman and restores her to her community, where before she was an outcast. In John 8:1–11, Jesus forgives a woman, restores her dignity, and calls her to stop sinning.

In the narrow understanding of salvation only one relationship is healed—the relationship between us and God. And it's like a legal transaction. Like I spent all my money and now my bank account is zero because of my sin. But Jesus is loaded, so I switch bank accounts with him, and now I'm loaded on paper. But nothing's changed in my actual wealth status. It's some special dealing within the cosmic skies. God is changed because God has forgiven me, but I haven't changed because the underlying problems remain. I'm still addicted to substances, addicted to online shopping, or still gossiping all the time because I haven't learned about the whole full-blown salvation available to me. Jesus doesn't just want to get me or you to heaven; Jesus wants us to be set free in our lives right now. To find healing in all of our relationships: the broken relationship between us and God, us and others, us and our inner selves, and us and the physical creation.

I'm not saying that restoring our relationship with God isn't important—it is. I'm also not saying that someone who is dying, someone who doesn't have a chance to change their behaviors, won't receive salvation and go to be with

Jesus if they ask for forgiveness on their deathbed. I believe they will.

But it's a sad thing to suffer through the pain of broken relationships while here on earth when we don't have to—the pain of not being able to love yourself, the pain of hating others, the pain of a broken relationship with the physical world. Jesus cares about those pains too.

We don't do good things just to secure our future. No. We do good deeds because we've been changed from the inside out. Living free from our addictions can become natural for us. We live this way because we're free.

The freedom isn't one hundred percent effective. Sometimes the old, sinful Michele raises her ugly head, and I do bad things. I'm a work in progress, and Jesus is still transforming me. I'm getting freer all the time.

Ephesians 2:8–10 can help us out here. Verses 8 and 9 say, "For by grace you have been saved through faith, and this is not your own doing; it is the gift of God—not the result of works, so that no one may boast." These are beautiful words. God's grace is really that free. But it's also God's grace that we have been created for good works. Verse 10 continues, "For we are what he has made us, created in Christ Jesus for good works, which God prepared beforehand so that we may walk in them."

I think Jesus wants to help us do good works because it's so much fun. Because it's free.

When it comes to embracing a broader view of salvation, an experience early on in my adult life made the difference for me. You see, I had a bit of a breakdown when I was a young married woman. Because even though I was part of a wonderful and gentle church growing up, I somehow absorbed the idea from the larger Christian culture to worry about doing things to please God and "secure" my salvation. Could I really trust that Jesus loved me just as I was?

One day I just gave up. I sat on the floor and cried and said, "I can't do this Christian life." And I felt God's love in a deep way right at that moment. The Spirit worked through people in my church who told me that salvation is a process as well as a first step, that it's more than just saying the sinner's prayer. I found a spiritual director. All of those things were salvation for me, gifts from the Spirit to help me in my journey of faith.

TOPICS IN CHAPTER 6

- The church is born
- One God, three persons
- God's new people: all are invited
- Conversion
- God's intervention in our lives

STORYLINE

- Jesus returns to heaven
- The day of Pentecost
- The early church
- Peter's vision and Cornelius
- Paul's conversion

6. God's Spirit Moving

IT LOOKS LIKE AND FEELS LIKE it's all said and done. Jesus lived, died, rose again, and ascended to the right hand of God. In some ways the problem seems solved. But if the story stops here, we leave the disciples cowering behind closed doors or fishing along lonely shores. They seem too afraid, too confused, to do anything. Is this what the new people of God are supposed to look like? The solution doesn't look like a good solution after all.

But wait. There's more to the story. Just before Jesus returns to heaven following his resurrection, the disciples ask him: "Lord, is this the time when you will restore the kingdom to Israel?" Jesus responds by getting them to look beyond their own nation. "It is not for you to know the times," he said. "You will receive power when the Holy Spirit has come upon you, and you will be my witnesses in Jerusalem, in all Judea and Samaria, and to the ends of the earth" (see Acts 1:6–8). Jesus tells the disciples to wait. Even though Jesus has died and come back to life, other things need to happen. The disciples need something more.

Something supernatural happens when we say yes to Jesus. Jesus comes to live inside us (Galatians 2:20) and we are forever changed. Isn't that what we talked about earlier—a change of identity? Isn't that the Holy Spirit?

If there is only one ethnicity gathered in the upper room for Pentecost, has God's solution really happened? I don't think so. God wants a people out of all people groups.

Wind, flames, and speeches

So, they waited. On the Jewish festival of Pentecost, they were all together to pray, as many as one hundred and twenty people (Acts 1:15). They were waiting—waiting for what, they didn't know. Suddenly, there comes a sound like a tornado, filling the house. Just as suddenly come little flames of fire, resting on each one of the people present. They look at each other. Can you imagine the fear and overwhelm? Then they begin to speak in other languages, tongues they don't know, speaking to everyone who will listen about the wonders of God. The Holy Spirit has come (Acts 2).

In one sense, these Jewish believers had no idea what was going on. In another sense, they did know. The strong wind reminded them of the wind that parted the Red Sea in the exodus (Exodus 14:21). The fire on their heads recalled the pillar of fire (Exodus 13:21). The different languages reminded them of the Tower of Babel (Genesis 11:1–9). Only this time, certain outcomes were reversed. Instead of bringing confusion and separation like the different languages did at the Tower of Babel, the Holy Spirit brought clarity and understanding. Foreign Jews visiting Jerusalem for the Pentecost festival heard words about Jesus in their native tongues.

A whole new kind of understanding. What phenomenon was so great that it reversed the effects of the Tower of Babel and came with all the symbols of the exodus? The Holy Spirit has come upon them. With this rush of mighty wind, there is a new being, an unexplainable presence among them, inside of them. It is the presence of Jesus.

Everything is different. Men and women who once cowered behind closed doors now preach in loud voices on the street

Trinity:
the classic belief among Christians that God exists in three "persons": Father (Creator), Son (Jesus the Redeemer), and Holy Spirit (Sustainer)

God is One, but we experience God in different ways. Christians have long believed in the Trinity, or held the understanding that God, Jesus, and the Holy Spirit are the same God in three persons (see Matthew 28:19–20; Acts 1:4–5; Romans 5:5–6; 2 Corinthians 13:13). That is, they share the same nature or essence. The Spirit and Jesus were both involved in creation (Psalm 104:30; John 1:3). Just as Jesus is God incarnated in human form (see p. 78), so also the Spirit is God's presence among us (John 16:4b–15; Acts 16:6–7).

See the Confession of Faith summary of Article 1 about God on page 183.

See the Confession of Faith summary of Article 3 about the Holy Spirit on page 183 and Article 18 about Christian spirituality on page 185.

corners (Acts 3:11–26). The ones who scattered after the crucifixion now live together as community, sharing food and possessions (2:43–47). With boldness, they heal the sick (3:1–10), preach repentance (2:38), and care for each other in radical ways (2:44–45; 6:1–7). They find themselves carrying on the work of Jesus in their own lives, in the strength of his Spirit.

The Holy Spirit's work was only beginning. Even though Jesus, through his life and death, defeated evil and made possible the solution to the sin problem, that solution had not quite reached its full potential. As the early disciples saw things, God's salvation was designed mainly for the Jews. It would take another series of events before they would remember how God called Abraham so that all peoples could be blessed (Genesis 12:3). It would take some special events for them to remember even Jesus' own teaching that God loved non-Jews as well as Jews. In a nutshell, the whole book of Acts is that story of how God's ultimate plan begins to unfold: the creation of one people from all ethnic groups and backgrounds (Luke 3:4–6; Revelation 5:9–10).

A whole new way of seeing things. It started in a rather small way. In a bizarre vision one day, God instructs Peter to eat animals that good Jews considered unclean to eat (Acts 10:9–15). Peter is stunned. This vision is asking him to go against everything he believes is right and good. He is already stretching his comfort level by staying at Simon's house (a man himself unclean because his occupation as a tanner involved touching dead animals). But this request of God? To *eat* unclean animals was to disobey God.

At the same time, in a town not far away, a Roman centurion named Cornelius also received a vision. In it, God instructs him to send for Peter. What a dilemma! Peter's understanding of what it

Who is the Holy Spirit? Jesus tells us in John 15–16. First, the Spirit is the Advocate (15:26). An advocate is someone who speaks on your behalf. This verse also says that the Spirit comes from the Father. Second, the Holy Spirit is the Spirit of truth. The Spirit helps us know truth; the Spirit testifies to what God wants (15:27). The Spirit will "prove the world wrong about sin and righteousness and judgment" (16:8). The Spirit will guide us into truth, speaking only from the heart of God (16:12–13). Finally, the Spirit will glorify God (16:14).

meant to be a faithful Jew forbid him from entering the house of a Gentile like Cornelius. Nevertheless, Cornelius sends his servants on this strange mission.

Meanwhile, the unclean animals keep descending in Peter's vision. A second and third time, a voice from heaven says, "What God has made clean, you must not call profane." Then, with perfect timing, just as the servants from Cornelius approach the house, the Spirit speaks to Peter, telling him to go with them

When the Spirit nudges

While I was working on a new book, I was struggling, not knowing what to say, wondering if God could even use me to write. Then I suddenly heard a voice.

It was 10:30 at night and the office building was locked. Nobody could get in. But it was my friend Neil. He had this strange look on his face. He said, "Don't laugh, but I think God sent me here." He was walking home, saw my light on, and felt God telling him to go see me. He said to God, "If the door is open, I'll know you want me to go see Michele."

The most amazing thing was that the door should have been locked, and yet he walked right in. We checked the door and sure enough, it was locked from the outside. There was no way he should have been able to get in. Now I believe firmly that the Holy Spirit spoke to Neil that night, instructing him to encourage me, even though Neil didn't even know what I was doing. Nothing spectacular happened as we talked, but I just felt this presence, this love of God pouring over me. God cared enough about me to send a friend at the right time.

That's what makes following Jesus so exciting. I think God wants to whisper in our ears and have an ongoing intimate conversation with us, where God prompts us to go and see a certain person or to send a note of encouragement to so and so.

Voice A: So, does the story in Acts 10 apply to questions of difference in the church today, like affirming people who identify as LGBTQ? Say more.

Voice B: The Holy Spirit was telling Peter not to call certain things unclean even if they were called unclean in the past. The metaphor for unclean used here is that of a pig. God told Peter to eat pork, which is off limits for many people groups.

Michele: Yes, and Peter took the food example God gave him and applied it to a Roman centurion. Within minutes of the vision about eating pigs sent to him by God, Peter met some servants of Cornelius, a military captain who wanted to be part of God's people.

Voice A: And Roman centurions would have been considered unclean?

Continued on next page

Michele: Yes, but not in God's eyes. And this event became the catalyst for the inclusion of the Gentiles into God's people—as Gentiles. According to Acts 15, the early believers decided that the Gentile men didn't need to be circumcised or become Jewish before they could become Christians. And a major factor in this decision was Peter's experience with Cornelius.

Voice A: So, one of the Old Testament laws, circumcision, doesn't apply anymore. And if the Spirit can make that kind of change back then, can't the Spirit do that now with Old Testament laws about homosexuality?

Voice B: Yes, but circumcision was just a ritual.

Voice A: We might think so, but back then, the Jews saw circumcision as a big deal. It was not just a little law but a big one. An identity marker.

Michele: If I hear you right, this is your logic: The Spirit—God—can do a new thing. The Spirit of God has authority over the Scriptures even for a big deal like circumcision.

Voice A: Yes, that's what I'm saying.

Voice B: But here's the problem with that logic: you could apply it to almost any situation you want. Let's say you want to start robbing banks. Hey, I just had a vision and the Lord told me it was okay now.

Voice A: No, that's not the same. Robbing banks clearly hurts others. Here we have a situation where the Spirit is saying, "Look, don't call unclean what I have called clean." I think people who are part of the LGBTQ community are clean in God's eyes. They always have been.

Voice B: Just because God did this with circumcision so that the Gentiles could be included in God's people doesn't mean God is doing that for LGBTQ people necessarily. To use this story to come to a conclusion of affirmation and inclusion is scary because it's so subjective. How can I argue with you if you say, "Well, the Spirit told me . . ." How am I supposed to respond to that?

Michele: Peter certainly had a change of heart. He says in Acts 10:34–35, "I truly understand that God shows no partiality, but in every people anyone who fears him and practices righteousness is acceptable to him." And the Gentiles started speaking in tongues. So, there's your proof that they had the real thing and that God accepted them—as Gentiles. I can understand the fear many have. If the Holy Spirit can reverse, so to speak, some parts of Scriptures, then yes, that might feel scary. But are we supposed to be governed by fear or by the Spirit? I think the issue underneath the acceptance of LGBTQ people is how we view the Scriptures. Is the Bible the Word of God or is Jesus the Word of God?

Voice A: So, you don't think the Scriptures are inspired?

Michele: I didn't say that. I love the Scriptures, and they are authoritative for my life. But I think we have to allow for the Spirit to show us a new thing, right? Is God really God or not? Let me put it another way. It's precisely because I honor the Scriptures as inspired—including this story where God declares something true that's really difficult for the Jewish believers to accept—that I have to admit that God can do that today too. God can declare queer people as beloved, made in God's image and acceptable just as they are, exactly like God declared Gentiles were acceptable just as they were in Acts 10.

without hesitation. All these miraculous things combine to help Peter experience a new conversion, a conversion to a brand-new understanding about God. "I truly understand that God shows no partiality, but in every people anyone who fears him and practices righteousness is acceptable to him," he says when he meets Cornelius (Acts 10:34–35). And while Peter speaks, the Holy Spirit descends on Cornelius and all who were hearing the gospel there. They begin to speak in tongues. This was proof beyond a shadow of a doubt. All people could become a part of the people of God.

A whole new kind of a church. Word of Cornelius's conversion reached the other Christians—one hundred percent of whom were Jewish, remember—and many did not know what to make of the whole thing. It became an even bigger question as Paul and Barnabas, sent by believers in Antioch, began to travel to other regions and attracted more Gentiles to the Christian faith. The pressing question for the church now was: How would Gentiles become part of the church? Did the men need to be circumcised? Put another way, did people need to become Jews first before they could be true Christians? Some Jewish Christians were actively teaching that they did, but Peter's experience with the vision seemed to indicate otherwise. Paul and Barnabas, who had seen many Gentiles turn to Christ, also argued vigorously that it shouldn't matter.

As Acts 15 tells it, the leaders of the church finally gather together in Jerusalem to discuss the new situation. There is a lot at stake. Would there be two kinds of Christians—Jewish Christians (first-rate) and Gentile Christians (second-rate)? What do Gentiles need to do to become part of the church? Are ethnicity and religious rituals (like circumcision) important for salvation, now that

Circumcision

In ancient times as well as today, males were circumcised, which means each man had a surgery that removed the foreskin of his penis. God asked Abraham to have this surgery done as a grownup, a painful commitment for Abraham to make. But this was part of the covenant or formal agreement God was making with Abraham (Genesis 15). Abraham was circumcised and afterward, circumcision became an important ritual for Jewish boys. Circumcision functioned as a physical sign that a male was part of God's people.

In the time period of the New Testament, most Gentile (non-Jewish) men were uncircumcised. So, the question up for debate was whether or not Gentile men needed to be circumcised before they could be followers of Jesus. Undergoing this surgery, in essence, meant becoming Jewish.

the church proclaims that Jesus is Lord of all people? What will this new people of God look like?

A major decision of inclusion. The believers at the Jerusalem conference prayed. They heard stories of what God's Spirit had done among Gentiles. They tried to discern the truth together. And they decided in the end that there would only be one church and that anyone could be a Christian without becoming a Jew first. The Gentile male believers did not have to be circumcised (undoubtedly to their relief!). From that moment on, Paul, Barnabas, Timothy, and others were sent on new mission trips with new freedom to welcome Gentiles around the world into God's new community. (The problem of "Judaizers" didn't go away, as indicated by Paul's letters, which often argue against those who wanted to insist on circumcision or to make Gentile Christians second-class.)

What an incredible feat! God's original plan, God's original desire starting with Abraham and Sarah, was now fulfilled. People who normally hated each other were eating at the same table, praying together, and staying in each other's homes. The new people of God came from every tribe and nation, and all of them were equal in God's eyes. That's what Paul meant when he wrote about there being no Jew or Gentile, slave or free, male or female in the church (Galatians 3:28). That doesn't mean that ethnic, social, and gender distinctions disappeared. But they no longer formed boundaries of who's better, or who's in and who's out.

Think of some examples in which people you know have been changed positively through their encounter with God.

A whole new creation. God wanted to—and did—create not only a beautiful physical world, but also a people as well. God dreamed of a people whose identity was not in their family line but in their saying yes to God—a community built on trust and obedience.

This is what Paul writes about in 2 Corinthians 5:17 (NRSVCE): "So if anyone is in Christ, there is a new creation: everything old has passed away; see, everything has become new!"

Some people see this new creation as only an individual, personal conversion. It's true that when we begin to follow Jesus and accept the mercy and grace he offers us, something new is created within us. But even more, Paul is talking about the church as the new creation. This new creation is a radical new way of living here on earth as God's new people. When the church is living as God intended, people who are normally enemies should worship together (Ephesians 2:11–22). Racial and gender identity, social status, and religious backgrounds aren't meant to cause division anymore. This radical way was incredibly good news in Paul's ethnically and socially divided society, and it continues to be so for us as well.

Salvation involves both the individual and the church. The early Anabaptists understood the importance of individual faith (see chapter 9). They understood that each person had to make his or her own decision to follow Jesus. At the same time, baptism made you a part of a community of people who supported each other, cared for each other, and had a common commitment to live the Jesus way together. They didn't believe that you could live the Christian life by yourself.

See the Confession of Faith summaries of Articles 9 and 16 about the church on pages 184 and 185.

Continued miracles

Because of the Holy Spirit, the church grows by leaps and bounds (Acts 2:41). Miracles continue (5:12–16). The believers voluntarily share their possessions and money, some selling everything and putting the money in a common pot (4:32–37). They open up their

Voice A: How do we know we have the Spirit?

Voice B: We do things we can't do on our own, like speaking in tongues and preaching and healing people.

Voice C: And the other, less flashy gifts of the Spirit, like being an encourager or a helper.

Voice A: But you can fake some of that stuff. Some people are charlatans.

Voice C: And some of us do have the Spirit but—I don't know—my gifts aren't apparent yet.

Michele: So, what's the true test? It's a great question. Paul answers this, I think, in 1 Corinthians 13. He says that the way you know you have the *real thing* is if you have divine love. Here are his words in verses 1–3 in the NRSV: "If I speak in the tongues of humans and of angels [speaking in tongues], but do not have love, I am a noisy gong or a clanging cymbal. And if I have prophetic powers, and understand all mysteries and all knowledge [a great preacher or teacher], and if I have all faith so as to remove mountains but do not have love, I am nothing. If I give away all my possessions and if I hand over my body so that I may boast [even being a martyr] but do not have love, I gain nothing." You can't fake real love.

Voice B: You can for a while, but eventually, people see through you.

Michele: I think Jesus says it like this in Matthew 5:43–48: "You have heard that it was said, 'You shall love your neighbor and hate your enemy.' But I say to you: Love your enemies and pray for those who persecute you, so that you may be children of your Father in heaven, for he makes his sun rise on the evil and on the good and sends rain on the righteous and on the unrighteous. For if you love those who love you, what reward do you have? Do not even the tax collectors do the same? And if you greet only your brothers and sisters, what more are you doing than others? Do not even the gentiles do the same? Be perfect, therefore, as your heavenly Father is perfect."

Voice C: In other words, children act like their heavenly Parent. And God who sends rain on evil people loves enemies just as we're called to do.

Voice B: Yes, and if you can't love your enemies, then your faith is probably worthless, because even nonreligious people can love their friends.

Voice A: We can't love our enemies without the Spirit inside us. That's the true test.

Michele: Salvation involves both the individual and the church. Nobody understood the importance of individual faith as well as the Anabaptists (see chapter 9). They understood that each person had to make his or her own decision to follow Jesus. At the same time, baptism made you a part of a community of people who supported each other, cared for each other, and had a common commitment to live the Jesus way together. Early Anabaptists didn't believe that you could live the Christian life by yourself.

homes as places to host church gatherings and put up traveling preachers (16:15).

Have you joined the community of the Spirit, the church? If so, what signs of the Spirit do you see there?

Paul's transformation. One of the biggest proofs that God was doing extraordinary things was a man named Saul, also known as Paul. Saul was a devout Jew, a Pharisee, which meant he had a particular idea of what the Messiah would be like. He wasn't that different from us; we all see and understand God through the lens of our background and culture. Saul, however, felt God wanted him to oppose this new Jesus movement. Jesus couldn't be the Messiah, Saul thought, because the Bible said that anyone hung on a tree was cursed (Deuteronomy 21:23).

One day, while on his way to the city of Damascus to arrest more believers, a great light suddenly shone all around Saul. Blinded, he fell to his knees. "Saul, Saul, why do you persecute me?" said a voice from thin air. "I am Jesus, whom you are persecuting" (see Acts 9:1–19). From that instant on, Saul knew that Jesus was the Christ. He knew that he had met the risen Lord. In the following days and years, more of the pieces fell into place as he learned the story of Jesus. But most importantly, Saul now followed Jesus as passionately as he had opposed him before. Saul—who then became known as Paul—became the greatest promoter of Jesus in the first century, to both Jews and Gentiles.

Not every person's encounter with Jesus was so dramatic. Other people, like Nathaniel, came to follow Jesus after much thought (John 1:43–51). Some, like Peter, said yes impulsively, then struggled with that commitment (21:15–19). Today, too, the Holy Spirit works with each of us in unique ways. Some experience dramatic conversions. Some feel like they've always loved and followed Jesus, as much as they know how. Some weigh the pros and cons,

Voice A: If the Spirit leads us into all truth, then why do Christians disagree with each other on so many issues? Everyone claims they're listening to God, but their conclusions are not the same.

Michele: It's not as easy as it sounds to hear the Spirit because sometimes the Spirit is telling you to stop being so obstinate. When in doubt, be humble, read the Bible—all of the Bible, not just a few choice verses—and talk to other Christians. And check your life. Are you living out the fruit of the Spirit? Watch for genuine love, joy, peace, patience, kindness, generosity, faithfulness, gentleness, and self-control (see Galatians 5:22–23).

Voice B: Sometimes it seems like the Bible disagrees with itself on issues.

Michele: When that happens, Anabaptists Christians ask this question: What did Jesus say about this issue?

Voice A: Why do they do that?

Michele: Because we believe Jesus uniquely reveals God and God's purposes for humans. The prophets and writers of the Old Testament described God and God's purposes in a variety of ways (Hebrews 1:1–3). But Christians believe that Jesus reveals the fullness of God and God's purposes (John 1:14). If anyone knows what God wants, it's Jesus, God's son. So, when the Bible disagrees with itself, we can look to Jesus for resolution.

or the proof, more than others do. All, though, can take a beginning step of faith in what will become the most beautiful, thrilling journey there is.

Our choice to transform. After we begin this awesome journey of faith, the path is never predictable. Sometimes we know the Spirit is speaking to us and at other times we wonder if it's just indigestion. Some Christians know immediately what their mission in life or their spiritual gift is, while others wait patiently and wonder. The hardest times to be faithful can be when you don't particularly feel the Spirit at all. Does that mean the Spirit isn't there anymore? No. It simply means that Christianity is more than our feelings and that the Holy Spirit moves freely.

We can't program God the way the Canaanites tried to program their Baal gods (see p. 69). The Holy Spirit is anything but predictable, except for this one thing: the Spirit of Jesus is here to help us,

How have you noticed the Spirit calling you either to begin a relationship with Jesus or to deepen your trust in and obedience to him? When have you wondered whether certain events or "nudges" in your life are the work of God's Spirit?

guide us, and love us (John 14:16–17; 15:26; Acts 9:31; Romans 5:3–5; 14:17; 15:13; Galatians 5:5, 22–23; 1 Thessalonians 1:6–7). The Spirit intends to change the world through us. The Spirit wants to do wonderful things through us, just like the Spirit did through the people in the Bible. On the other hand, the Spirit will never force us. The choice rests with us to be open and ready to move when the Spirit moves.

You may also feel discouraged when you see Christians—including yourself—fail to live up to their claims. How does that affect your confidence in the Holy Spirit?

Summing it up

- *Jesus lives on in us, the church, through the Holy Spirit.* As the early believers waited and prayed, the Spirit of Christ came and changed them into people who would take the good news—the Story—to the world. The Holy Spirit can work like that in us too.

- *God, Jesus, and the Holy Spirit are one.* The Christian belief in the Trinity helps us see how the presence and work of the Spirit in our lives today is really the continuing presence and work of Jesus. In Jesus, God has shown God's own self in our world. As we continue to say yes to Jesus, the Spirit moves into our lives and transforms us.

- *The Spirit works through the church.* The story of the church's beginning is really the story of the Holy Spirit. Christians don't live in isolation as individuals. The surest sign that we have the Spirit is the unity we experience with Christian sisters and brothers. The church is constantly growing and developing as God's new creation. But the Spirit works in each of us to build up the church and to build our character toward what God intends for us.

- *When the Spirit is present, human divisions break down.* The early church had to make a one-hundred-and-eighty-degree change in their thinking: Jesus had broken down every barrier to God, including ethnic barriers. Christian unity is a sign of the Spirit's work today as well.

A spiritual discipline to practice

Gather together with other Christians and brainstorm about the barriers that the church community might unintentionally be putting up. Who would feel unwelcome when they try to enter your community? Then, spend time in prayer and ask the Holy Spirit to speak to you and give you discernment. As you pray, listen for the Spirit to give you a task to do or perhaps a new person to call—some new opportunity for you to welcome others.

TOPICS IN CHAPTER 7

- God meets us where we are
- Salvation—another look
- Saying yes to the Story
- Steps to becoming a Christian
- Baptism
- Joining God's people, the church
- The Lord's Supper—communion

STORYLINE

- Our own lives
- Apostle Paul's letters

7. God's Story, My Story, Our Story

IN THE LAST SIX CHAPTERS we have pondered the Story of God in the world. The climax of that story was and is Jesus. And like all who have met him in person, we must decide for ourselves how to respond to Jesus. "Who do you say that I am?" Jesus asked Peter in Matthew 16:15—and he asks the same of us. Jesus longs for us, like Peter, to say that he is the Messiah, the Son of the living God. He longs for us to leave our fishing nets and follow him.

I'm tempted to make salvation very simple—and in some ways it is very simple. I want to emphasize having a relationship with Jesus. Getting up every morning, knowing I'm God's child. The Master of the whole universe wants to talk to me, change the world through me.

Scratching where it itches

In the New Testament, Jesus uses many ways to help people find what they most need. Some people have their physical or social needs met as they come to Jesus (such as the widow in Luke 7:11–17). Some people have their whole worldview turned upside down when they meet him (Nathaniel in John 1:43–51 or Paul in Acts 9:1–22). Often, Jesus declares forgiveness to those who feel an overwhelming burden of sin (Simon Peter in Luke 5:1–11). For the woman caught in adultery, Jesus says, "Neither do I condemn you. Go your way, and from now on do not sin again" (see

In some ways, becoming a Christian is a personal decision that only you can make for yourself. No one should push you into this. In other ways, becoming a Christian means joining a group of people, letting them help you figure out how to follow Jesus and figure out how to do life.

John 8:1–11), giving her grace and calling her to holiness all at the same time.

holiness:
1) a way of expressing the total otherness and purity of God; refraining from sin and imitating God's own character
2) being set apart or called out by God for a special job (Leviticus 20:26)

grace:
kindness and mercy, which we can do nothing to earn

A rich young religious leader who had done everything right in his life still felt a spiritual restlessness. To him, Jesus says, "Go and sell your possessions" (Luke 18:18–30). But in the very next story about another rich man, Zacchaeus, Jesus doesn't say, "Zach, give up your cheating ways." Instead, he says, "I must stay at your house today" (see Luke 19:1–10). Out of that experience of hospitality, Zacchaeus's life is transformed. Somehow Jesus knew what each person needed to hear. He knew that Zacchaeus needed to hear grace, while the only hope for the young leader lay in the hard call to leave his wealth.

It's that way for us, too. Jesus knows exactly what we need and offers us salvation in the way that fits our need. Some of us, if we're honest, need a good jolt. We're prideful and full of ourselves. So the words of Jesus might sound abrasive to us, but down deep, we know they ring true. Others of us are so filled with shame for things we've done that we can't even look Jesus in the eye. For us, Jesus offers such love and gentleness that we can find

Voice A: I didn't have a dramatic conversion experience. Is that a bad thing?

Michele: I think that's fine, but a big conversion experience can also be okay. Jesus comes to us in different ways.

Voice A: I hear you, but sometimes I wonder if I really have "the real thing." How do you know for certain? I asked Jesus into my heart and got baptized and all, but I struggled afterward. Still do.

Michele: Salvation is a journey and baptism is at the start of that journey, not the finish line. It's okay if you can't pinpoint a date when you decided to follow Jesus. Depending on a person's personality and family background, some people desire a big conversion experience while some need a more gradual approach to commitment.

And it's okay to struggle with certainty when it comes to salvation. It takes a lifetime to become more and more like Jesus.

freedom and forgiveness and, in that, find the power to leave our sin behind.

You may not have heard about salvation in ways that are helpful to you. Unlike Jesus, fellow Christians can't know completely what you need. But that's one reason why there are so many different pictures of salvation in the Bible—they speak to our varied needs as humans, in all our complexity.

What we can say with assurance about salvation

For all the different pictures given to us in the Bible, there are some common threads that run through them.

It's a relationship thing. Remember the stories from Genesis that help define the problem of sin (pp. 34–37)? Salvation mends and heals all the relationships that sin breaks—our relationships with God, others, ourselves, and all of creation. This makes salvation so much more than just believing in Jesus. Yes, we do believe in Jesus, but it's the kind of "believing" that affects and changes our whole life—including our relationships.

If salvation means following Jesus in a relationship, then that means it is ongoing. When we first say yes to Jesus as Savior and Lord, it is a beginning, not an end. Some people think that as soon as they see their children or friends get baptized, they can wipe their brows and say, "Whoosh, I'm glad they did that," as if the baptism closed the deal and now they don't have to worry about their loved ones anymore. Like every other relationship, salvation is a journey.

It's a God thing. Salvation comes to us through God. In the story, God makes the first move—always. "While we still were sinners Christ died for us," writes Paul (Romans 5:8). We can have a relationship with God and be transformed because of the

Salvation is a matter of life and death. But that's different than believing it's only matter of life after death.

faithfulness of Jesus, not because we have such wonderful faith ourselves.

The Holy Spirit comes to each of us and—in different ways for different people—nudges us toward God. We can say no to the Holy Spirit; God does not coerce us into following Christ. But we take on faith that the Holy Spirit whispers to us what we need to hear, even if the message may be hard to hear (Luke 18:18–30).

When we do say yes, a supernatural, unexplainable, incredibly wonderful thing happens to us. This is the part of salvation that is hardest to understand. God changes us. God makes us into new people. The Holy Spirit lives inside of us *and* we find ourselves in Christ. God forgives our sins *and* begins to break the bondage of sin so that we are free to become what we were created to be. We have a new identity. We are transformed (Romans 6:1–14).

This happens whether we feel it or not. Christianity is more than a set of feelings. It's more than some emotional high that we sometimes get at camp or a big worship event—wonderful as that is. Since our experience with God is a journey, it will have ups and downs. And when our experience with Jesus looks different from the experiences of other Christians, it doesn't mean their experiences are real and ours are not. God is God, and not some cosmic pop machine. God works differently with different people as God sees fit.

It's an us thing. As much as it is a God thing, it is also an us thing. Jesus never forced anyone to follow him, and that holds for us as well. The Holy Spirit invites us to follow Christ and join God's people, and we must decide whether or not to accept the invitation. That is true even if we come from families who have been Christians for many generations. Each one of us has the privilege and the responsibility to say yes or no. It's true that if we're not careful, we can put so much emphasis on our part and our response that salvation becomes little more than good works that we use like a merit badge to get us into heaven. Salvation is still about *God* and God's work in and for us. But it is about *us* in the sense that we have to accept this wonderful gift that God offers us. We must dare to believe that Jesus loves us this much, that the Creator of this world wants to have a friendship with us, wants to care for us—out of love.

While salvation is an individual decision that only you can make, it's also a community thing. Part of the decision to become a follower of Jesus is to join God's people. It's true that we're the only ones who can choose to be in a relationship with Jesus; no one else should make that decision for us. But that decision also brings us into community with others who help us follow Jesus. We gather to worship God and pray together. We commit to figuring out the truth of the Bible together. We support each other when we're feeling down; we rejoice with each other in our victories. We share our possessions and money with each other. This is what it means to follow Jesus as a church.

repent:
to turn from sin and commit oneself to a change of life

It's a repentance thing. The bare-bones message that Jesus and his followers proclaimed was "The kingdom of God has come near; repent, and believe in the good news" (Mark 1:15). Meeting Jesus means you eventually also come face-to-face with your own worst enemy—sin. Like Peter when he first met Jesus, we come to the point of praying, "Go away from me, Lord, for I am a sinful man" (Luke 5:8). (Of course, Jesus didn't leave him; Jesus called Peter to follow him.)

Mennonite Christians are individualistic. We emphasize that each person must decide for themselves whether to follow Jesus. Yet we're also communal. We believe that the only way to know how to follow Jesus is by processing together as a local church.

Repentance, as it is understood in the Bible, means a lot more than saying "I'm sorry." Repentance means turning our life around one hundred and eighty degrees. It means reorienting our behavior to follow God's way, not our own. Such a turnaround is impossible in our own strength. But that's where the Holy Spirit works in us in supernatural ways, right from the moment we say yes to Jesus. Would the Story be good news if we had to remain in our sin for the rest of our lives? Would it be good news if we didn't ask and receive forgiveness from each other and by God's help mend those relationships? No, our salvation starts right now, and that is such good news.

When we confront and confess our sin, God forgives both the bad things we have done and the good things we have failed to do (1 John 1:9). But God doesn't leave us there. The Holy Spirit gives us what we need to live lives that are radically different from the rest of the world. When everyone else looks after number one, we put the interests of others first (Philippians 2:4). When others dominate, we serve each other by washing each other's feet (John 13:1–20). When the rest of the world loves only those who love them back, we go beyond that standard and love our enemies (Matthew 5:43–48), not because we have to, but because that is who we are in Christ. That is how children of God act—just like their heavenly Parent.

It means Jesus is Savior and Lord of our lives. Sometimes we talk about Jesus as our Savior, and at other times we speak of Jesus as Lord. Both of these realities are important, and they work together in us. Remember that there is nothing—*nothing*—we can do to earn God's favor. We all mess up. We are all in need of the gracious gift of salvation that God offers us through Jesus. We can't save ourselves. Only Jesus can.

But Jesus must also be the Lord of our lives. Something or someone is lord when they have our first and total allegiance. Whatever is first priority is lord. At the time of the early church, people throughout the Roman Empire were required to declare "Caesar is Lord." If they refused to do this in a public setting, they could be arrested and punished. But for Christian believers, this was a dilemma. Jesus and Caesar could not both be Lord. Christians had to choose whom they would serve—sometimes at the risk of their own lives. Who would give them the most security? To whom would their loyalties go? What was the most "real" reality?

Saying "Jesus is Lord" won't get us killed today in Canada or the United States, but the choice is still the same. Jesus and government cannot get equal loyalty from us. We cannot put our ultimate security in both Jesus and the force of arms. To put anything else ahead of Jesus is to make an idol of it, to make it lord instead of Jesus. If and when the laws of our land contradict God's laws, we obey God first (Acts 5:29).

The tension goes even deeper than that. The dominant culture can win over our loyalty in subtle ways. If Jesus is Lord of our lives, then we have a different value system than the rest of the world. Contemporary society may say that one race is better than another, or one gender better than another. It might list things that make a person popular or cool, to which we say no! Jesus has different values. All races and genders are equal. Because Jesus was Lord in the early church and ethnicity was not, Jews ate with Gentiles, and those who were enslaved worshiped with those who enslaved them, which in time led to the enslavers freeing those who were enslaved. This kind of community was unheard of elsewhere in the world. It was a miracle as great as the crossing of the Red Sea.

It means being with God forever. What awesome news! Salvation starts now, and it continues after we die. We get to be

What things are we tempted to serve as our lord instead of Jesus? Some people are tempted by needing the latest clothes, or the pressure to be popular, or by putting our trust in the military for protection. Read and discuss the Confession of Faith summary of Article 23 on page 185 about where we place our trust.

in the presence of Jesus. The Bible speaks of a New Jerusalem coming down (Revelation 21:1–4) and all earth being renewed. We may not understand exactly how it will be, but it will be glorious. We will experience resurrection. Every tear will be dried. When times are tough, we can feel comfort in knowing this. A day will come when we will see Jesus (John 14:1–7; Philippians 1:21–26)!

Saying yes to Jesus

Until now, we have been describing salvation—the Story of God as it touches the world and as it touches our lives. In that description we've referred to some of the responses that this story calls out in us. If you're wondering what it takes to clinch that decision to follow Jesus, here is a summary:

1. *Choose God's Story as your own.* Out of all the ways of understanding who we are and why we are, we choose the story of how God has been loving and drawing us through Jesus Christ. Salvation is a love story, a love story where the Creator of the universe reaches out in incredible ways—even from the cross—to help us see that we are loved and to help us accept and trust this love. As we nurture this trust, this relationship, God's Story defines our identity and our way of looking at the world. We believe in Jesus and join the Story.

2. *Receive God's forgiveness and grace.* We all need to be reconciled with God. God, through Jesus, provides what we need to be forgiven and restored to a relationship with God. We experience that forgiveness as we repent—confessing our sin and asking God to empower us to live faithfully.

3. *Join God's people.* All along, God has been creating a people who follow in God's way. Salvation is not just an individual experience. It involves being part of God's people and joining in God's mission to the world.

4. *Follow Jesus with joyful gratitude.* We follow Jesus as Savior and Lord—not because we have to, but because we don't have to. In the strength of the Holy Spirit, we not only *can* follow Jesus, but we *want* to. We live in joyful gratitude for all God has done for us. It's the hardest thing and yet the most joyous thing all at the same time.

   Jesus explains this paradox in a parable from Matthew 13:44: "The kingdom of heaven is like treasure hidden in a field, which a man found and reburied; then in his joy he goes and sells all that he has and buys that field." Here we see great sacrifice. Someone sells everything she has—everything—to buy what seems to be a simple field. That is a lot of sacrifice. But this sacrifice is worth it because the field has a secret; it's filled with treasure. We followers of Jesus are the same way. Yes, we're sacrificing everything to follow Jesus. But it's a no-brainer sacrifice because there is no greater joy than to follow Jesus.

What is your experience of salvation? Have you had a dramatic encounter with God? Or have you come to faith more gradually?

Going public with baptism

Saying yes to Jesus may feel like an overwhelming step, but it is a wonderful, life-changing step too. Christians make that decision public through the church's ritual of baptism with water. People have a lot of questions about baptism. Is it *just* a ritual? Does it have some power to bring us salvation? Do we have to be baptized to be a Christian or to live with Jesus after we die? Is it something you are supposed to do at a certain age because that's the tradition in our church?

Baptism and Anabaptism

The step of baptism has always been an important event for Anabaptists, the branch of the Christian church that includes Mennonites. *Anabaptist* literally means "rebaptizer." In the 1500s in Europe, Anabaptists rejected the state church's practice of baptizing all infants in the society. For Anabaptists, baptism signified a personal decision to follow Christ, a decision that would be impossible for a baby to make. Anabaptists looked at the Bible and could find no examples of infant baptism. What they did find were stories of people receiving baptism as evidence of their commitment to Jesus.

The Anabaptists, therefore, rebaptized believing adults who had already been baptized as infants, and they refused to have their own babies baptized. This civil disobedience was a threat to the state church and government. Infant baptism was part of the process of becoming a citizen. Refusing infant baptism defied the state's authority, and, even more importantly, it messed up the government's system of counting people for taxation.

By not baptizing their babies, Anabaptists weren't trying to avoid paying taxes, but they were making the statement that church and state should not be one and the same. A citizen of Germany, for example, should not automatically be considered a Christian. If that were the case, then the best way to spread Christianity would be to conquer other governments by force and make people Christians by making them citizens of the state. (This was how Christianity often did spread beginning in the fourth century, when Christianity became the official religion of the Roman Empire. Later, during the Crusades, "Christian" soldiers made their captives become Christians at the point of a sword.)

See chapter 9 to learn more about the Anabaptists. Also, see the Confession of Faith summary of Article 11 on page 184 about baptism.

Here are a few things that the Bible says about baptism:

Baptism is a sign of faith. On the day of Pentecost, those who welcomed Peter's message about Jesus were baptized and added to the company of Jesus' followers (Acts 2:41–42). Baptism in the New Testament is always associated with repentance and faith.

Baptism is an aid to faith. Baptism symbolizes and reminds us of our new life in Christ (Romans 6:1–4; see the significance of the modes of baptism below). Like other rituals, baptism has no special power in itself and it doesn't guarantee a miracle or a spiritual high. But neither is it an empty practice without meaning. Rather, it helps open us up to experience God in a new way.

Baptism shows obedience to God's call. Jesus himself was launched into his mission in life at the time of his baptism. In baptism we show our readiness to participate in carrying God's story forward (Matthew 3:13–17). Jesus instructed his disciples to go and make disciples throughout the world, baptizing and teaching them to observe his teachings (Matthew 28:19–20).

Baptism is a pledge. Baptism shows publicly that we are prepared to be part of the body of Christ, or the church (Galatians 3:26–28). This new life with God will be lived out in the context of a local congregation. It is a commitment to faith, accountability, and ministry (Romans 6:1–11).

Baptism is not a rite of passage. Being baptized isn't like getting a driver's license at age sixteen. There is no standard age or grade in school for baptism. Instead, it needs to happen after we have made our own commitment to Jesus. That happens at different ages for different people.

Baptism is not recognition of achievement. Baptism isn't a sign that we have passed a faith exploration class or that we are now spiritually mature. Baptism is a sign of what God has done for us in Christ, not what we have achieved for God.

Different styles, different pictures of God's work

Sprinkling, pouring, and immersion are three forms of baptism that have been practiced in the church over the ages. Each way has biblical foundations, and each one emphasizes a special aspect of salvation.

- *Sprinkling* reminds us of the Jewish sacrificial system. The priests would sprinkle the blood of an animal against the sides of the altar (Leviticus 7:2; 16:14). Christians took this ancient ritual and applied it to Jesus in Hebrews 10:22: "Let us approach with a true heart in full assurance of faith, with our hearts sprinkled clean from an evil conscience and our bodies washed with pure water." When the baptismal water is sprinkled over new believers, it pictures their cleansing from sin and guilt through the death of Jesus.

- *Pouring* recalls the anointing of Jewish high priests as they were consecrated for service (Exodus 29:7). In the New Testament, God "poured out" the Holy Spirit (Acts 2:17, 33; 10:45; Titus 3:6). When water is poured upon baptismal candidates, it pictures the coming of the Holy Spirit in their lives and their complete dedication to serving Jesus.
- *Immersion* symbolizes death and resurrection. Baptismal candidates are dunked in a tank, a lake, or some other body of water and then raised back up out of the water. The Israelites came through the Red Sea, leaving behind their old lives of slavery and rising to their new freedom as God's people. The apostle Paul talks about believers burying their old, sinful lives in baptism and rising to new life in Christ (Romans 6:1–4; 1 Corinthians 10:1–2; Colossians 2:12). Peter connects baptism with Noah's flood, which "buried" a sinful world (1 Peter 3:19–21). And so today, immersion can be a symbol of our death to sin and our rising to new life through Jesus.

Voice A: Is it okay to be immersed when you are baptized? Do you *have* to be immersed?

Michele: That's a great question. I think it is okay but I don't think you have to be. If the metaphor of dying with Christ and then coming back to life is especially meaningful to you, then let's get you to a lake! Baptism has a wealth of symbolic meaning: being cleansed, the Spirit being poured on you, dying to your old self and coming back to life in Jesus. Different methods of baptism emphasize different meanings.

Baptism and the Holy Spirit

The New Testament speaks of Christians being baptized by one Spirit (1 Corinthians 12:13). Water baptism and the coming of the Holy Spirit are closely connected, even though the Bible doesn't show a particular sequence of events. When Jesus is baptized, the Holy Spirit rests on Jesus right at the time of his baptism (John 1:33). In the book of Acts, some people receive a baptism of special signs of the Holy Spirit before they are baptized by water (Acts 10:44–48). Others receive water baptism first (Acts 8:14–16). The Holy Spirit comes to us in unique ways as we say yes to Jesus. The Spirit gives us special gifts for ministry as we do God's work (Ephesians 4:1–16; 1 Corinthians 12). The Spirit also produces the fruit of love, joy, peace, patience, kindness, generosity, faithfulness, gentleness, and self-control (Galatians 5:22–23).

Joining a family of faith with church membership

For Mennonites and many other Christians, baptism is connected with becoming a member of a local congregation. We cannot live our Christian lives as islands to ourselves. Saying yes to Jesus makes us part of a spiritual family of followers. That family is always a group of real people, not some symbolic association. God is still creating a cohesive people, not a bunch of individuals with their tickets to heaven. We need each other for support, accountability, and help in discernment. The apostle Paul talks to the Corinthians about being God's "temple" (1 Corinthians 3:16–17) and the "body of Christ." Both are pictures of something made up of many parts that depend on each other.

See the Confession of Faith summary of Article 9 on page 184 about the church.

The church is not a club. Membership in a church is different from membership in a club. In today's society, we are flooded with offers to be a member of some club. "Membership has its privileges," one credit card company says. Becoming a member of most organizations is a breeze. You pay the dues or you do one special little thing, and you're in. Most people join because it benefits them. Many want their clubs to keep "undesirable" people out.

Membership in the church is not meant to be like that at all. No one can be kept from being part of God's people because of racial

Voice A: What about church membership? Should baptism automatically make you a member? Doesn't this create conflict like infant baptism and the state-church union?

Michele: How so?

Voice A: To me, either you have a relationship with Jesus or not. I don't see the need for church membership. And nobody's persecuting us, no king is trying to kill us, so, do we really need the church?

Michele: I think we need the church. God chose to save us by becoming a human and walking among us as Jesus. So, the truth we're looking for is not found in a book, but in this God/human Jesus. And both two thousand years ago and today, the way to understand this Truth called Jesus is in relationship. Jesus chose twelve disciples and they walked with him for three years! And after Jesus ascended into heaven, they still gathered together in the upper room, trying to figure things out, praying for the Spirit to come. At the Jerusalem conference, the early Christians settled together the issue of whether Gentiles are considered in or out, simply by hashing it out. We need the church.

Voice A: But it's hard to be the church right now.

Michele: It is. There's no getting around that truth. But if Jewish and Gentile believers who had been brought up to hate each other could do it, we can too.

Voice B: I think part of the problem is that we have to redefine what unity means. Maybe it's not agreeing completely on a set of beliefs, but being willing to love each other in community no matter what.

Michele: Not only do we need church, but I'm a fan of membership too. I think it's important because I think it's hard to be a Christian all by yourself, even in modern times when we're not being persecuted. We need each other for encouragement and critique and to hold each other accountable.

Voice B: What if some people want to be members of the church, and yet they need more time to think about whether they want to be baptized?

Michele: I think a person can be involved in church life and that experience itself can help you determine whether you want to be baptized. But it seems strange to me for a person to want to be a church member who isn't committed to Jesus and a public statement of that commitment by way of baptism.

Voice A: But what does being a church member even mean nowadays?

Voice B: And what if a kid wanted to be baptized at age seven? Can they be a good member of the church that young?

Michele: I was seven when I went forward to receive Jesus at a revival meeting. Perhaps I was too young to know what I was doing, but on the other hand, I was earnest in my love for Jesus. My sweet congregation took me seriously. I took baptism classes twice in a row, and at age nine, I was baptized. And yes, I was a member in full standing. I've never regretted a single moment of my early commitment, but that's just my story.

Voice A: Okay, I love Jesus and I want to be baptized, but I'm not sure I want to be a part of a congregation.

Voice B: Why not?

Voice A: Because they don't live what they say they believe. People are hypocrites.

Continued on next page

or gender identity or economic status. Membership is free. At the same time, the standards of the church are higher than any other group. It may cost you everything—even your life. That doesn't mean that you will die when you become a church member or that you will have to give up all your money automatically, but in some times and places, it has meant just that. (This was true for the original Anabaptists in the sixteenth century.)

And we don't join a local congregation to get something, even though there are benefits to being part of the church. We join a church because that's who we are in Christ. We do it as part of our worship and obedience to God. Just think how different some worship experiences might be if people came with the desire to *give* something instead of expecting to *get* something.

Michele: Maybe you can help them with that. Just because the church is flawed doesn't mean Jesus doesn't want to use it to heal the world.

Voice A: But I can have a relationship with Jesus without the church.

Voice B: Maybe, but who's going to keep *you* from becoming a hypocrite?

Michele: When we see a congregation struggling to follow Jesus, as we define it, which might not be perfect either, it's a golden opportunity for us to be self-aware, to ask the hard questions about what's not going well, and through the Spirit—change. Then people will want to join us.

Voice B: Some people, myself included, felt pressure to get baptized at age twelve. As far as I'm concerned that's just delayed infant baptism if people are getting baptized because it's the general expectation or to make their parents happy.

Michele: I agree that no one should feel pressure to do something they're not ready to do. Baptism isn't some magic pill we take and then—boom, we're good. And while baptism doesn't save you, I still think it's an important thing to do, a step that Jesus calls us to do. I feel this way about church membership too. Just like we've been talking all along, following Jesus is about relationships. Humans are built for relationship. Jesus wants to use us together to be a true people of God formed out of all people groups, to bring salvation to the world.

I need to be in relationship with people who disagree with me completely. But it's hard. And I need to shed tears with and hear the stories of people who challenge me. But what if they're right? What if they can see something I can't see?

The Lord's Supper as food and drink for the journey

The church's combination of high standards (living Jesus' way) and open membership may seem strange. Yet, what holds the body of Christ together is love. This incredible love is celebrated and nurtured in what we call the Lord's Supper, or communion. In this ritual, Christians gather to remember and proclaim the death of Jesus.

As Jesus did with his disciples on the Thursday night before his crucifixion, we eat bread and drink wine (or grape juice, in many churches) (Luke 22:14–23). We remember the exodus, when God freed a group of enslaved Israelites from Pharaoh's oppression. We especially celebrate the new reality that Jesus introduced. The broken bread is a sign of Christ's body, which was broken on the cross. The wine is a sign of Christ's blood shed for us. As we eat the bread and drink the cup, we recognize Jesus' presence, and we open our hearts in a fuller way to Jesus and to each other.

Jesus spoke of the bread and the cup as signs of the new covenant that God makes with us through his death (Matthew 26:28; Mark 14:24; Luke 22:20). Like the earlier covenants in the Old Testament, this final covenant comes through God's initiative and out of God's love for the world. As often as we take communion, we reaffirm our own side of the agreement: we say again that we want to live in the way of Jesus.

Confession and forgiveness as the "each other" part of communion. We can say all the right words and respect the ritual of the bread and cup, but if there is a major economic inequality in our church community or if we have a grudge against someone else in the church, we might as well not do communion at all (1 Corinthians 11:17–22, 27–34). We must take care to get rid of economic hardship, resolve conflicts among ourselves, confess our sins to each other, and ask and offer forgiveness. Only together can we be the body of Christ (1 Corinthians 12). Without love for each other, the ritual of communion is empty and we do not experience the Spirit of Jesus within us (1 Corinthians 13; 1 John 4:20).

Washing each other's feet as a sign of love. In many Mennonite communion services, this love for each other is expressed also through the footwashing ritual. Just like communion and baptism, footwashing cannot bring us salvation. It does not automatically produce love in us. It's not a requirement of being a Christian. (Not all Mennonite groups have this tradition.) Yet it can be a way of reinforcing our call to lay down our power and serve others. God placed all things into Jesus' hands (John 13:3), and yet on the eve of his crucifixion, he laid it all aside as he demonstrated his love by washing the disciples' feet. He told them, and he tells us, to do the same (John 13:14).

See the Confession of Faith summaries for Articles 12 and 13 on page 184 about communion and footwashing.

Summing it up

- *Salvation is both an event and a journey.* It is a transformation that God initiates in our lives and to which we must say yes. It is completely free, yet costs us everything. It changes us instantly, and yet we keep on being transformed for the rest of our lives. What a wild and beautiful paradox to live into!
- *Baptism, communion, and footwashing are signs of God's work in us and in the world.* They symbolize the story of God's saving deeds in our world, especially in the life, death, and resurrection of Jesus. They are also signs of our response to the story.

Think about all the times in your life when you have watched or participated in baptism, communion, or footwashing. What have they meant to you?

- *Baptism represents God's action of forgiveness and salvation; it also marks our commitment to following Christ.* Baptism is also associated with the coming of God's Spirit into our lives.
- *Communion is a sign of God's covenant sealed in Jesus' death on the cross.* It also is a sign of our participation in that new covenant.
- *Footwashing is a ritual that reinforces our call to serve each other in love, as Jesus did.*
- *We cannot follow Jesus alone.* When we declare our commitment to Jesus in baptism, we become part of the church—a family of faith where we can exercise our gifts and give and receive support for our faith journey.

What does it mean to be a disciple of Christ? Having started the journey, what are the next steps along the way? We'll explore these last questions in the next chapter—but take a few minutes to think about them now.

A spiritual discipline to practice

Practice being the body of Christ together. Get together with three to six others and commit to a time of sharing about God's work in your lives. To make things easier, have a bag of small household objects to use as prompts (picture, matches, pencil, comb, silk flower, eraser, etc.). Ask each person to pick one object to help him or her share, choosing one of these statements:

- I saw God this week when . . .
- The one miracle I would love to have is . . .
- If I could change one thing in my life right now . . .
- If I could change one thing in my church, it would be . . .
- I need your prayers for . . .

TOPICS IN CHAPTER 8

- "Watering" the Christian life
- Spiritual disciplines
- Inner life
- Outer life
- Sharing good news
- Exercising spiritual gifts

STORYLINE

- Our own lives

8. Living Into the Story

A GOOD FRIEND OF MINE ONCE SAID, "Faith is like planting a tree in Kansas. Commitment is like watering it every day." I understand his point. Kansas is dry. It's windy. It's downright beastly hot in the summer. You can feel silly planting a tree in the middle of a prairie, where it seems like nothing but prairie dogs thrive. But while it might take some courage to plant the tree, it really takes gumption to water it day after day after day.

If you have surrendered your life to Jesus and experienced baptism—or are planning to be baptized—you have "planted the tree." It took faith—as much faith, perhaps, as it takes to think a tree will grow on a prairie. But now that it's planted, what does it mean to "water" your new life? You have entered the Story. Now what does it mean to live into it?

Watering isn't always fun, but having a tree on the prairie is wonderful. Sometimes nurturing our life with God seems like hard work, but experiencing God is fabulous. In this chapter we'll discuss spiritual disciplines and the exercise of our spiritual gifts. Those are things that don't just happen; they require something of us. Yet as we cultivate and water, our Christian lives can be as satisfying as a cool drink of water on a hot summer day—under the shade of a huge tree.

Voice A: Does God still speak to people like he did with Abraham and Sarah? I want to believe this. I'm scared to believe it, though, because I've listened for the Spirit's voice and I haven't heard anything.

Michele: Believe me, the Spirit is moving in the world in a mighty way. Keep listening. You won't be disappointed!

Voice A: Can I be honest? Sometimes church is boring. I felt super close to Jesus after I was baptized, but two weeks later, church felt same old, same old. Why bother?

Voice B: Are the spiritual disciplines supposed to be fun all the time? Soccer practice isn't fun all the time, but it's how I get better at the game I love.

Voice A: Yes, but you shouldn't have to pretend. Going to church and all the other things have to eventually get you somewhere. And you've got to be real with God. If it's boring, it's boring.

Voice B: Can you do something that makes church less boring? What's the Spirit telling you to do?

Michele: Our Christian lives are like sailing a boat. We put up the sails so that we can catch the wind. The wind may or may not be blowing that day, so even though we put up our sails, we may not go very far. God is like the wind, and putting up the sails is like our spiritual disciplines. We can't force God's hand by putting up our sails, but if we don't spend time in prayer, for example, we won't catch the wind no matter how hard it blows.[8]

The early Christians had to learn how to water their faith. People we read about in the book of Acts said yes to Jesus, were baptized, and became part of the church. That was only the beginning. The earliest Christians experienced conversion, but the transformation wasn't done. Just like the disciples before them, these new believers had to learn to walk with Jesus. Their problem *and* their advantage was that Jesus, no longer visible to the eye, was now experienced through the Holy Spirit. Sometimes that was very powerful and real (Acts 4:31), and at other times it took more faith than they seemed to have. That's why they kept meeting together for prayer, teaching, and support (4:32–34).

One telling story involves a teenager whose faith seemed further along than that of her elders. A group of believers were praying for Peter's delivery from prison. But when the prayer was actually answered and Peter showed up at the door, none of the believers could believe it—except Rhoda, a teenager. She kept insisting that the real Peter, not his ghost, was at the door. Finally, they checked for themselves and let him in (Acts 12:6–17).

We don't have to, but we do want to. As it was for the early believers, so it is for us. When we become Christians, we become different. Jesus talks about our being "born again" (John 3:3 NIV), and Paul talks about God's people being a "new creation" (2 Corinthians 5:17). We gain a new identity. We do things that some people may find difficult to understand: we love our enemies and spend time in prayer because *not* to do them would be strange in God's scheme of things. How can we not do what is in our very nature to do?

Then the question is, if the Holy Spirit is bringing all these changes now that I'm a Christian, what do *I* need to do? Living the

Christian life is hard to explain. The being and doing are all mixed up (James 2:14–26). We don't have to earn our salvation—we can't, and in that sense, we don't have to do things like praying and going to church. We can't do anything to win God's approval. God's love is a gift of undeserved love, grace. At the same time, if we have a true relationship with the Holy Spirit, then we start to change from the inside out, and because of that transformation, we behave differently. Our faith is brought to completion by our works (James 2:22). We do good deeds, we act in a different way, because we are being transformed into a new person.

God's gift of grace is real, and if we are not careful, we can come dangerously close to believing in what has been called "cheap grace." Cheap grace is a distortion—when people think that they can live undisciplined Christian lives because God will always love and forgive them in spite of conscious sin.

If we have experienced God's grace, we find ourselves wanting to love God back through our lives. We find ourselves *wanting* to exercise spiritual disciplines and get our lives in line with God's will. Thus we'll do the work of watering and cultivating our faith, even when it's not glamorous. The simple discipline of going to church, for example, isn't absolutely wonderful all the time, but we understand that something beyond instant gratification is there. Does that seem too far-fetched? Disciplines have a purpose and a joy beyond themselves. As Richard Foster writes in *Celebration of Discipline*, they transform us. They make us effective for the journey of faith.[9]

Spiritual disciplines: habits of the heart

In Mark Yaconelli's chapter in the book *Starting Right*, he writes, "Spiritual disciplines are the *means* through which believers seek to respond to God's invitations of love. They are the habits, disciplines, and patterns of life through which we seek communion with Christ and solidarity with others."[10] The following is a list of habits and practices that help water the tree of our Christian life. Some are more central than others.

No one may truly know Christ,
except one follows him in life.
And no one can follow him,
except he [or she] know him.

—**Hans Denck**,
early Anabaptist leader[11]

Voice A: I'm not sure I believe in miracles.

Voice B: Any miracles?

Voice A: I'm not sure. I think you can take all the miracles of Jesus and see them as spiritual lessons that teach us something. So, the stories have worth, but the miracles themselves probably didn't happen.

Voice B: I think they did. I think Jesus healed people in a supernatural way. And why even bother to pray if you don't believe in miracles?

Voice C: What is the purpose of prayer? Is it to get God to do something for you that wouldn't happen otherwise? Or is it to help you feel better?

Voice A: Or do you pray so you can know God's will better? Isn't prayer supposed to be more about listening than talking?

Michele: Can prayer have all of those purposes? Maybe, depending on how the Spirit helps you to pray, you sometimes ask for a direct miracle and God says yes. Other times, God says no, or later, or something else. Even in the midst of asking God directly for a miracle, you are also giving the situation to God. You essentially say, "Whatever you want, God." This reminds me of Mary's faithful response to the angel Gabriel. The angel said, "For nothing will be impossible with God" (Luke 1:37). And Mary shows us how to submit to God's purpose in prayer. "Here am I, the servant of the Lord; let it be with me according to your word" (Luke 1:38).

Prayer. Prayer is talking with and listening to God so much that we start to think God's thoughts and desire what God desires and love what God loves. Then, when we ask God for something specific, which is our usual definition of prayer, God gives us what we ask for—because God has also given us the right desires (Psalm 37:4; John 16:23–24).

Bible study. God wants to replace old, destructive habits of thought with new, life-giving habits. What we fill our minds with determines what kind of habits we form. God wants us to know—and live—and be changed by the Story. We study the Bible with an open heart and with others, for no one is so smart or so objective that they can discern the truth alone. In fact, arrogance is the death of this discipline. We study the Bible in its cultural and historical background so that we can understand the meaning it had for the original audience; then we apply it to our situation. We memorize Scripture so that the words become deeply ingrained in us.

The Lord's Prayer

Our Father in heaven,
hallowed be your name,
your kingdom come,
your will be done,
on earth as in heaven.
Give us today our daily bread.
Forgive us our sins
as we forgive those who sin
against us.
Save us from the time of trial
and deliver us from evil.
For the kingdom, the power,
and the glory are yours
now and forever. Amen.[12]
—Matthew 6:9–13

Community worship. Just as much as we need alone time with God, we need time together with other believers. The early believers met daily to worship together (Acts 2:46). When we worship together in a local congregation, we can support each other, encourage each other, and hold each other accountable.

Service. "So if I, your Lord and Teacher, have washed your feet," Jesus told his disciples, "you also ought to wash one another's feet" (John 13:14). Service is the spiritual discipline whereby we "wash each other's feet." This may mean helping someone paint her house or volunteering in a homeless shelter or prison. But true service goes a lot deeper than outward actions. Ironically, the outward actions can be a stumbling block to true service. We can feel so good about what wonderful servants we are that we put ourselves above the ones we serve. True service helps us get rid of self-righteousness. True service helps us be humble. It breaks apart all pecking orders and dashes our typical ideas of leadership.

Simplicity. Simplicity sets possessions in their proper place. It's not that things are bad in and of themselves; it's just that they're not God. Simplicity is really an inward reality—seeking God's

---

Voice A: I can play violent video games and not automatically go out and kill someone.

Voice B: Yeah, but, little by little, doesn't playing those games dehumanize certain groups of people for you? Doesn't it affect you just a little bit?

Voice A: It probably does, but they're so fun.

Voice C: Is Jesus asking us to give up all social media? R-rated movies?

Voice B: We are to be "in the world, but not of the world" (see John 17:11, 14–16). What does that even mean?

Michele: Jesus doesn't expect us to not interact with the culture and society we live in, but we must have a different loyalty—a loyalty to Jesus first. And we see reality in a different way because of Jesus. So, we can have smartphones and social media profiles, but we must use these things in a different way from others. We are supposed to continually seek God's kingdom and constantly try to bring God's healing to everyone. In that way, we are in but not of this world.

kingdom first and finding true joy there. That results in the outward reality of being free from worry over materialistic things. You can take them or leave them (Philippians 4:10–11).

The discipline of simplicity also speaks to us about our use of time. Our schedules can become so busy we hardly have time for anything other than endless work! What does that say about where we are putting our ultimate trust? What freedom is there when we are slaves to our schedules? As Richard Foster has said, the purpose of spiritual disciplines is freedom—freedom from the enslaving habits of sin, freedom to be mature in Christ, and freedom to place ourselves before God so that God can transform us.[13]

Fasting. Fasting is the discipline of refraining from something—usually food—in order to focus more directly on God. The Israelites would fast for two reasons: to repent, usually as an entire nation (Esther 4; Joel 2); and to prepare themselves for receiving the spiritual strength to complete a hard task. Jesus fasted in the wilderness (Matthew 4:1–11). When we go without food and grow hungry, we begin to realize our dependence on God. Fasting disrupts the rhythm of life. It creates enough disequilibrium in our lives that we become more sensitive to God's quiet voice speaking to us.

Silence and solitude. Many Christians practice spending time alone, without talking to people or engaging with other distractions for a specific amount of time. This quiet time creates a space for God to speak to them. Rather than loneliness, solitude brings an inner fullness that is actually the best medicine for our deepest longings. We can't run away from ourselves anymore, and when we can finally face ourselves—with God to help us, the joy is overflowing.

Voice A: Is it sacrilegious to be angry at God?

Michele: Not according to the book of Psalms, where 70 percent of the psalms are laments, meaning poems that express sadness or anger toward God. It seems like it's okay to shake your fist at God in that book anyway! It is also true that, when we sit down and listen, sometimes the Spirit helps us recognize that our suffering is not God's fault, or to see that we don't have the whole picture. But you have to be able to be angry at God because all real relationships are honest. We have to trust that God loves us enough to want all of our emotions and thoughts, even the angry parts.

Journaling. Journaling is writing our prayers and thoughts out on paper. More than writing in a diary and not quite penning an essay, journaling helps us reflect on God, listen, and sort out what God is trying to say to us.

You have to focus on the kingdom of God or spiritual disciplines can become legalistic. How do you keep the practices of the Christian life from becoming ends in themselves rather than means to grow in your relationship with God?

Confession. If we believe God loves us even though we mess up, we can bear to admit and repent of our sins. If we don't examine our lives as part of being a healthy Christian, we will tend to blame others when something really is our fault. We will make excuses that keep us from finding the freedom from sin that we need. So we must examine our lives, sometimes with the help of others, to figure out what is out of alignment and how we can restore it. We confess our part of the mess. With the help of the Holy Spirit, we change our behavior. And through this process of confession, we feel God's love.

Forgiveness. The other side of confession is forgiveness. Others have hurt us. Now the bondage is not only the pain of our own hurt, but also the anger we feel toward those who have hurt us. To work toward freedom and healing, we must either forgive those who have hurt us directly, or "for-grieve" them, to borrow a phrase from David Augsburger's book *Helping People Forgive*.[14]

If the person who hurt us recognizes his or her fault and confesses it to us, we can work to forgive that person. God has forgiven us, and, as the Lord's Prayer reminds us, we experience God's forgiveness as we forgive others. As Jesus instructed, we are to forgive "seventy times seven" (Matthew 18:21–34).

When the wrongdoer is not willing or not available to confess, we can "for-grieve" them. In doing so, we release those hurts to God, we ask for healing, and we move on with our lives. Ideally, for-grieving happens after we have attempted to be reconciled with the other person as much as possible. But sometimes reaching out to someone who has harmed us is not safe. Protecting ourselves from further harm is also a way to honor God.

Even when people do ask for our forgiveness, sometimes the hurt goes so deep that it takes many years for us to forgive, or forgiveness may not be fully possible in this life. That's okay, as long as we are working at it with God's help. God is with us each step of the way.

What spiritual disciplines have you made habits in your life? Which ones would you like to strengthen?

Practicing the disciplines

The above disciplines are the most common, but there are others, such as spiritual guidance, intercession, hospitality, and submission. Some of those listed, such as prayer, Bible reading, and forgiveness, are pretty essential to practice. Others, such as journaling, may be more fitting depending on our personalities and are optional. Whichever ones we choose, we will be most healthy in our Christian lives if we keep a balance in three areas: being alone with God, connecting with other believers in the church, and serving in the world beyond ourselves.

Each of us may develop a slightly different mix of disciplines and practices. But all believers are called to let God transform us at all times. Being a Christian means living differently from the rest of the world and letting God shape our values. Our salvation affects our ethics (our sense of what's right and wrong). We treat our families with respect and love. We live according to the Bible's high standards for sexual purity. We don't cheat on tests. We don't gossip or spread lies. We care about and befriend unpopular kids in school. Why? Because we are God's people and because we are in Christ and our whole identity has changed as a result. We are different. And it shows.

disciple:
one who is committed to learning from Jesus; one who follows the way of Jesus even at great personal cost

Words and deeds attract others to Jesus. Because we are different, people around us will take note. When they hear the Story, including how we entered into it, they will be curious. When they see how we are being transformed to be like Christ (1 Corinthians 2:16), they may want that transformation as well. When they hear how we experience God in prayer and see how we love our enemies, they may say "Count me in!" This is why Peter writes that every Christian should be prepared to give an answer to everyone who asks you to give the reason for the hope that you have (1 Peter 3:15). See the Confession of Faith summary of Article 10 on page 184 for the importance Mennonite believers place on mission.

---

ethics:
principles of human conduct, with respect to the rightness or wrongness of actions and the goodness and badness of motives and ends

God's people—from Old Testament times to today—are called to spread God's good news to an ever-widening circle (Matthew 28:19–20). This is evangelism: sharing the good news of Jesus and inviting others to begin a relationship with Jesus. We share the good news with others because we are experiencing it ourselves and are able to recommend it to others. When that happens, we're seeing the Story advance. Abraham and Sarah were told they would be a blessing to all the people of the earth. Today God wants to bless others through us.

Discovering your spiritual gifts

Everyone who says yes to Jesus has a mission. Every new believer—just like Abraham (Genesis 12:3), Lydia (Acts 16:11–15), and Barnabas (Acts 4:36–37; 9:26–30; 11:22–30)—gets a supernatural tap on the shoulder and hears a voice in the ear saying, "Have I got a job for you!" The apostle Paul writes about the church as a body in which each part, each organ, has a unique role (1 Corinthians

12:12–26). Paul calls these jobs "gifts"—abilities from the Holy Spirit that help build up God's people and complete God's work in the world.

In 1 Corinthians 12:8–11, Ephesians 4:11–16, and Romans 12:5–8, Paul lists several of those jobs as he talks about the work of the church. Putting those lists together, the jobs include serving as apostles, prophets, evangelists, pastors, or teachers; compassion; exhortation; giving; leadership; speaking in tongues; interpreting tongues; healing; miracle-working; faith; and discernment of spirits. All of these—and many others—help to build up the church until all people come to unity, maturity, and "the measure of the full stature of Christ" (Ephesians 4:13).

Voice A: I'm not comfortable evangelizing to people. I don't want to push people into anything. I think we can be so different from non-Christians that they notice us and want to know what's up. And then we need to have the words ready to talk to them.

Michele: I like the idea of discipling people more than the stereotypical image of evangelizing people. How do we help each other become mature Christians who turn right around and disciple other people? How do we keep that cycle of discipleship growing? How do we do it in an authentic way that doesn't feel awkward? Maybe we need to work more on becoming mature Christians first and then this will all make sense.

Cautions for spiritual gifts

First, recognize that your spiritual gift is not for you. It is for the church (Ephesians 4:12) and for the continuation of God's Story in our world. Second, all gifts in the church are different, yet equally important. When Paul compared the Corinthian church to a human body in 1 Corinthians 12:15–26, he emphasized that diversity was good; not everyone can be an "eye," for example. And every gift in the church was needed, just as a body needs each part; what would we do without a nose?

Third, unless the gifts are exercised in love, they are useless (1 Corinthians 13:1–2). Paul had to get right in the faces of some church members who thought they were hot-stuff spiritual giants because of their gifts. Ironically, the more arrogant they became, the more they showed how spiritually immature they really were.

Fourth, we can be too timid about using our gifts. Some Christians look at their young age or their lack of experience and education and they think, *Wow, I can't do that*. But God is not necessarily concerned with age or education. God wants people who are available and desire to serve God. As Richard Foster demonstrates in *Celebration of Discipline*, a longing for God is the primary requirement for practicing the disciplines and using our gifts.[15]

Like Mary, who was asked at a young age to be the mother of Jesus, we each have a calling. Like Paul's young coworker, Timothy, we are each called to serve, knowing that the one who made the blind see is the same one working in and through us. God can and does work through each person who says yes to Jesus—sometimes in miraculous ways, other times in ordinary ways.

It can be difficult to believe that God does want to use us, but I assure you that God does. We know this through the story. The story tells us that God wants to interact with us, whether through our spiritual disciplines or through our gifts, so that we can experience more of God. Every day, every hour, we must look for God, expect God, and listen and watch for God. At the same time, we believe in God even when we don't feel a thing and there seems to be no evidence that God is even around.

Remember, practicing our faith is like watering a tree. You can't see the tree growing. Day after day it looks just like a little twig poking out of the ground. But you keep watering, and suddenly one day you realize it's on its way to being a giant oak tree. How did this happen? Your watering every day did not make the tree grow on its own—God did the rest. By watering the tree, you helped provide the environment where it could grow. As we practice spiritual disciplines, and as we practice using our spiritual gifts, our faith grows. We experience God in ever new and wonderful ways. We are transformed.

What is a spiritual gift that you are discovering or exercising? How do you work at finding out what gifts God has called you to use for God's kingdom?

Is God trying to whisper something to me?

Michele: If you could petition God for something that you know would help you in your Christian life, what would you ask for?

- For God to strengthen my faith when I'm not feeling his presence.
- For help in trusting God during difficult times.
- For people to be brave enough to talk about polarizing issues and listen to each other.
- For people to be real at church.
- For us to do church outside sometimes.
- For adults to tell their faith stories.

Summing it up

- *As Christians, we practice spiritual disciplines.* There are many ways of explaining why we do so, but it comes down to this: we are followers of Jesus Christ. We nurture and deepen that relationship as we practice life-giving habits. We water the tree, and it grows healthy and strong.

- *Our salvation impacts our behavior.* Every day, in big and small ways, we live differently because of Jesus. By the way we live, we reflect who we are and who we are becoming in Christ.

See the Confession of Faith summary of Article 17 on page 185 about discipleship.

- *We represent God to others.* God depends on Christians to announce to others, in words and deeds, the good news that God loves the world and offers healing and hope.

- *We are given spiritual gifts to help us live out our unique mission in life.* The Holy Spirit gives us spiritual gifts, which we in turn use to help build God's kingdom. Most often other Christians in the local church help us discern what our gifts are.

- *The Story continues.* The Story didn't end with the early church. God still wants to draw people from every walk of life into the people of God. Our next topic for discussion is how the Story has unfolded over time and how the Mennonites fit into it.

How do you feel about sharing your faith story with friends, especially those who are not Christians?

A spiritual discipline to practice

One of the basic and necessary spiritual disciplines is the practice of silence. Grab some paper and a pen and take one hour just to sit by yourself. Don't allow yourself access to a cellphone or any electronic device. If weather permits, spend the hour outdoors. Write down whatever comes to your mind. If nothing comes to your mind, just enjoy the rest and the quiet. Give yourself the grace of low expectations and spend time with God.

TOPICS IN CHAPTER 9

- The church throughout the centuries
- The Anabaptists
- Mennonites today
- Distinctive Anabaptist beliefs and practices
- The future end of the Story
- The Story continues in our lives

STORYLINE

- The church throughout the centuries
- New heaven and new earth (Revelation)

9. The Rest of the Story

IT'S WILD TO THINK WE ARE part of God's work in the world. Christians are part of something big—the church. This larger belonging is more than any denomination, such as Mennonite, Lutheran, Roman Catholic, or Ethiopian Orthodox. All those who have said yes to the Story and live in the Story—all God's people throughout the world and throughout history—are part of God's work. And the Story continues to unfold today.

Sometimes it's hard to remember that I am a part of a story so much bigger than me. I'm part of the people of God, millions strong.

During every period of the church's history, Christians have sought to follow Jesus. They longed to draw others into God's family by word and deed, by being a unique people that attracted the curiosity of those who had never heard of Jesus. Out of all people groups, the people of God loved their enemies, told others about Jesus, and sought to live out the teachings of Jesus by the help of the Holy Spirit. This people of God, now the church universal, is still doing this today.

From its earliest beginnings, the church spread to different parts of the world. When Christians faced persecution, they fled to safer places, and there they told their neighbors about Christ. Thomas is traditionally believed to have taken the good news of Jesus to India. Mark, one of the gospel writers, went to North Africa. Peter was martyred in Rome for his outspoken commitment to Jesus.[16] Usually the response to the gospel message was mixed. Many people joyfully became Christians, finding a whole new way of life. But others felt threatened by the message. Two hundred years after the resurrection of Jesus, Christians faced gladiators in Rome because of their faith. Fifteen hundred years after the resurrection, other believers were being executed for their commitment to follow Jesus and remain true to the Bible. Even today Christians face persecution, yet their genuine faith gives them the strength to continue in joyful obedience.

Even though the story of Christianity has continued on for more than two thousand years, the same issues have been at the heart of the faith. What does it mean to be followers of Jesus? Who is truly Lord of our lives? What does it mean to be part of the world and yet be citizens of God's kingdom? How should the church function in relationship to the government?

The answers to these questions have never been easy, but examining the history of the church can help us to wrestle with them. We look at the lives of Christians from other ages and other countries not to copy exactly what they did, but to learn lessons from them as we carry the Story forward in our own lives. With the help of the Spirit, we can not only learn what it means to be faithful, but to also have the courage to live it out. Let's consider how the Story has been lived out since Jesus' time.

Find out about the persecution of Christians around the world today. Go online and search to learn about people who face great hardship because they follow Jesus.

Voice A: So, the early church was perfect?

Michele: No, but through the power of the Spirit and the example of Jesus, they were able to live into the shalom that God has always desired.

Voice A: So why don't we live like that today?

Michele: Some Christians do.

Two thousand years of Christianity in a nutshell

The first three hundred years. Until the fourth century after Christ, Christians met mainly in each other's homes. They shared their possessions freely, cared for the poor among them, and welcomed everyone no matter who they were or where they came from. They were nonviolent, refusing to mistreat their personal enemies and refusing to fight in the Roman army.

During this time, Christian leaders and scholars began to write down their understandings about God and Jesus to guard against teachers and philosophies that corrupted Christian faith. They laid the groundwork for decisions about which documents—Gospels, letters, and other writings—had enough authority to be included in our Bible.

These first three centuries, however, were also difficult for the church. Because Christians called Jesus their Lord rather than Caesar, they experienced waves of persecution. Sometimes Christians were eaten by lions, sometimes crucified or burned on poles along the Roman roads. Persecution scattered the Christian movement farther throughout the known parts of the world; Christians established thriving communities on the continents of Asia and Africa. Persecution also made them stronger in their faith. By the end of the second century, the church often required new believers to take long periods of prebaptism instruction (often three years) in order to make sure they were ready for possible suffering. Despite great opposition, the church grew in number. As early church leader Tertullian said, "The blood of the martyrs was the seed of the church."[17]

The reign of Constantine. Much of this changed with Emperor Constantine in 313 CE. He was fighting in a battle when he saw a vision of a shining cross in the sky. He heard a voice say, "In this symbol, conquer." He told God that if he won the battle, he would become a Christian. He did win, and there was soon a total turnaround in the treatment of Christians. Through the Edict of

Christians . . . do not inhabit separate cities of their own, or speak a strange dialect, or follow some outlandish way of life. . . . With regard to dress, food and manner of life in general, they follow the customs of whatever city they happen to be living in, whether it is Greek or foreign. . . . And yet there is something extraordinary about their lives. They live in their own countries as though they were only passing through. They play their full role as citizens, but labor under all the disabilities of aliens. . . . Like others, they marry and have children, but they do not expose them. They share their meals, but not their wives. . . . They pass their days upon earth, but they are citizens of heaven.

—from a letter by a Christian, written between 150 and 180 CE[18]

Milan, the emperor now called for the toleration of all religions. It was only a short step until another emperor, Theodosius, made Christianity the *only* religion allowed.

At first glance, this seemed like good news—no more believers being fed to the lions. But Constantine's idea of making society Christian through the power of the empire was almost the death of the church. Now people were forced into being Christians, or they were automatically considered Christians because of their citizenship. As the church became "official," many Christians didn't even know that being a Christian meant living a transformed life, free from sin. Choosing to follow Jesus in obedient love wasn't even on the radar screen.

The centuries that followed were known as the Middle Ages. The Roman Empire crumbled, and yet the church continued to enjoy great power. In 1054, the one orthodox church became two: the Roman Church (Catholic) and the Eastern Church (Orthodox),

---

Michele: Throughout the centuries, God's people have been tempted to make God specifically "their" God. When they received a human king a thousand years before Jesus, the people of Israel started thinking they had a national God. Before that, anyone willing to worship the Lord could be part of God's people, but after the installation of a king, you had to be a citizen and live in the right land to be considered part of God's people. Jesus was tempted by Satan in the same way to use government control (or violence) to force people to follow him.

And about three hundred years after Jesus' ascension, Christians caved to the same temptation to conflate political power with religious identity. Being a good Roman citizen meant being a Christian even if you didn't even know who Jesus was, let alone follow him.

Now in North America, especially the United States, we have a subtle version of the same thing with the rise of Christian nationalism. In some people's minds, being an American and being a Christian mean almost the same thing.

Voice A: And so being a Christian means nothing different at all. Is that what you're saying?

Michele: Yes, you got it. If you believe that all Americans are automatically Christian, then people are just Christians in name only.

with both claiming to be the real church. The head of the Roman Catholic Church, the pope, often had more power over the state than emperors or kings. As the church gained more land, it soon became wealthy. Rich people thought they could buy their own forgiveness from sin by contributing to the church.

Soldiers went to the Middle East on a mission called the Crusades to recapture the Holy Land from the Muslim Turks. While some may have thought they were doing God's will, many others went simply to gain wealth and have an adventure. In the name of Christ, thousands of innocent people, including Muslims, Jews, and Eastern Christians, were plundered, killed, or "converted" at the point of a sword.

All was not bad in the Middle Ages, however. Monks and nuns who wanted to live out the teachings of Jesus lived together in community. They remained unmarried and became voluntarily poor so that they could devote themselves to prayer and service. They fed the hungry and cared for the sick. They copied the Scriptures from ancient texts. In many ways, they tried to bring the church back to what it was in the beginning.

The Reformation. By the 1500s, an incredible revolution was forming in Western Europe. Explorers from other lands brought new ideas. People rediscovered ancient writings, which made them question traditional religious ideas. Christian reformers like John Hus and John Wycliff called for common people to study the Bible for themselves. A man named Johann Gutenberg invented the printing press, which made it possible for people to buy books at affordable prices, including the Bible. With all these changes it became more and more difficult for the government or the church to control what people believed and taught.

Enter Martin Luther. This German monk, like so many others, was disturbed about the state of the church. He was especially bothered by the way spiritual favors were sold by an ever-richer Roman Church. In 1517, Luther wrote a stinging criticism of the state church and nailed it on the door of the church in Wittenberg. Arguing from the Bible, which he eventually translated into German, Luther preached that people are made right with God through faith, not by their efforts to please God or by the rituals of the church. Because of such *protest*, the movement Luther began was called the Protestant Reformation. The term *Protestant* still applies to non-Catholic, non-Orthodox denominations today.

The hierarchy of the Roman Church opposed Luther, but several powerful princes who agreed with his teaching protected him. His reforms were able to thrive in Germany and spread to other parts of Europe. Luther worked to give the new movement political power, so that the reformed churches would become state churches just as the Roman Catholic Church had been. Ironically, after these reformers gained their own religious freedom, they denied that freedom to others.

Ulrich Zwingli of Zurich, Switzerland, was one such reformer. He went farther than other thinkers of his day, daring to think of a church that could be somewhat free from the state. He even questioned the traditional practice of baptizing babies. But the government authorities of Zurich put pressure on Zwingli not to go too far in his reforms. Apparently infant baptism was still the best way to determine a head count of citizens for tax purposes and encourage people to be part of the official state church. Zwingli soon buckled and kept the link between church and state strong.

The Anabaptists. Several of Zwingli's followers did not buckle to political pressure. Conrad Grebel, Felix Manz, and Georg Blaurock refused to compromise what they understood from the Bible. They were convinced that the only way to experience the true church was to join God's people because you wanted to, not because you were born into it. They knew that membership in the church based on membership in the state was not real Christianity at all. Grebel and the others argued these points vigorously with the government officials, and they refused to have their own babies baptized.

At a meeting in January 1525, Grebel baptized Blaurock, and Blaurock in turn baptized Grebel and several others present with them. In that simple act, they defied their government and the state church, returning to the free churches of the time before Constantine. They, and thousands of other likeminded believers after them, began to meet informally as an alternative church. They also went everywhere, calling others to a personal commitment to Jesus.

These believers paid a heavy price for their actions. People made fun of them by calling them "Anabaptists" ("rebaptizers," since the first members had already been baptized as babies). The governments of Europe, both Catholic and Protestant, outlawed the movement, forcing the Anabaptists to meet secretly in homes and in forests. Thousands were tortured, run through with a sword, drowned, or burned at the stake. But despite the bloody persecution, the Anabaptist movement spread like wildfire through Switzerland, Germany, Holland, and other countries in Eastern and Western Europe.

Though there were variations among the different groups of Anabaptists, Michael Sattler and other leaders hammered out seven important beliefs they could agree upon. This document became known as the Schleitheim Confession. Its main points follow:

- The rejection of infant baptism as a means of salvation
- Keeping the church pure by banning members who had strayed from their commitment and refused to change (see Matthew 18:15–20; this was in contrast to the state, which used violent physical punishment for breaking church or state rules)
- Understanding the Lord's Supper as a memorial of Jesus' death, not as a ritual where the bread and wine become Christ's body and blood (as the Catholic Church believed)
- Separation from the world's values
- Laypeople as congregational pastors and leaders
- Nonresistance, including the refusal to bear arms
- Forbidding the swearing of oaths

What beliefs would you be willing to die for?

True evangelical faith cannot lie dormant. It clothes the naked. It feeds the hungry. It comforts the sorrowful. It shelters the destitute. It serves those that harm it. It binds up that which is wounded. It has become all things to all people.

—**Menno Simons**, 1539[19]

Menno Simons. One of the most important leaders of the Anabaptists was a man from Holland named Menno Simons. Menno began his career as a Catholic priest. For years, he struggled with many doubts about the state church's practices. Even more, he was bothered that his fellow church leaders based their beliefs on church tradition, not the Bible.

At that time, some Anabaptists in Germany adopted some bizarre beliefs, including the use of violent force to establish their movement. In 1536, after hearing about these misguided beliefs, Menno knew that he must leave the state church and join the peaceful Anabaptists. Soon he became a recognized leader of the Anabaptists. Always stressing the importance of interpreting scriptures through the life of Christ, he helped them distinguish truth from wrong teaching. Eventually, many Anabaptists became known as "Mennonites."

Mennonites on the move until today

Intense persecution of Anabaptists continued through the sixteenth and early seventeenth centuries. Eventually they settled into close-knit communities where they could practice their faith in peace. Often because of their refusal to join the military or bear arms, Mennonites had to migrate to countries or regions where service was optional. They migrated to many parts of Europe, Ukraine, and North and South America. Sometimes they moved because they were directly persecuted and in danger for their faith.

North America became a refuge for Mennonites from the persecution and rising militarism of Europe. At the invitation of William Penn, a group of thirty-four Mennonites and Quakers from Germany arrived in America in 1683 after a ten-week journey across the ocean. Settling in Germantown, Pennsylvania, this group made the first formal protest against the slavery system in America. Soon, thousands of other Mennonites, primarily from Switzerland and South Germany, moved to Pennsylvania and then on to Ohio, Indiana, and further west. Others went north to Ontario.

When the Mennonites settled in North America, they were also displacing peoples who were already there. Indigenous peoples were forced off their lands by European Americans in a process called colonialism. In colonialism, a group seizes political control and takes land away from the original people groups, exploiting them to gain the land for themselves. Europeans who came to America assumed they could just take the land. They killed Native Americans or purposefully broke the land agreements they made with them. Having removed the Native Americans, they claimed the land to be free or cheap for the taking. Mennonites benefitted from this injustice. Most of them never asked why the land seemed empty; they simply took advantage of the opportunity to purchase cheap farms. Today, many Christians are wrestling with this reality and contemplating how to right the wrongs done to our Indigenous siblings.

Even though Mennonites believe in nonviolence as a key teaching of Jesus that applies to our lives, they sometimes don't live out this teaching very well. In 1534, a group of Mennonites tried to set up their own government in the city of Münster, Germany, leading to violence. And during World War II, some Mennonites joined Hitler's forces and supported the Holocaust. They chose to give primary allegiance to their government, and thus participated in a great atrocity. These stories are painful to tell, but it's important that we remember every part of our history, to learn from it and to ask the Spirit for the strength and wisdom to follow Jesus completely.[20]

My great-grandfather had to choose between serving in the army and being tarred and feathered. He understood that it was the government's right to punish him, but he trusted God to take care of him. One afternoon, men came with buckets of hot tar. When they got about three feet away from him, they stopped in their tracks, cried out, dropped their buckets, and ran. No one knows for sure what they saw or why they ran. But my great-grandfather believed that God protected him that day.

From the beginning, the Mennonites lived among other groups of people. Mennonites who migrated to North America did not have their own land reserve as Mennonites in Russia did (see below). So, they had to figure out how to relate to people who believed differently than they did and at the same time preserve what they believed in. Many chose to isolate themselves from the wider culture by dressing differently and speaking their European languages instead of English. In the United States, the Revolutionary War of 1776 and the Civil War of 1861 were testing times for the Mennonites, but also opportunities to strengthen their faith. The Civil War forced the Mennonites to rethink their teaching on nonresistance. Many suffered persecution for not serving in the military.

The Mennonites who went to Russia to escape persecution have an especially moving story. Beginning in the 1780s, Mennonites moved to West Prussia and made prosperous colonies there. The Russian government gave them much freedom, including religious freedom and exemption from military duty. But within a hundred years, those freedoms started fading. When the Bolshevik Revolution came in 1917, the colonies were in true danger. They were attacked by armies on both sides and by others jealous of their wealth. Famine struck. Hundreds of Mennonites died. Many were able to flee to Canada and the US, but many others were forced to stay. Some were sent to Siberia where they faced forced labor, cold, and hunger. During World War II, many Russian Mennonites were able to flee to Europe, then went on to settle in North America and several countries in South America.

Even in modern times, many Mennonites are under pressure from their societies and governments. In 1982, the Ethiopian Mennonite Church, known as Meserete Kristos (Christ the Foundation), was outlawed by the Marxist government. They had to go underground and suffered intense persecution for nine years. But God blessed them during this time of hiding and persecution. When religious freedom was granted again in 1991, Meserete Kristos realized that they now numbered fifty thousand, a tenfold increase of their membership prior to their persecution.

Mennonites in mission

In the late 1800s, Mennonites in North America, Russia, and Holland began to look outward again. Like many other Christian groups, they felt a new call to fulfill Jesus' final instructions to make disciples of all nations (Matthew 28:19). Missionaries started churches in Indonesia, India, Democratic Republic of Congo, China, Argentina, Colombia, Ethiopia, and many other countries. As they shared the good news of Christ, they also served human needs by establishing hospitals, schools, orphanages, and economic development programs. Mennonite missionaries did not always have intercultural awareness, and some of the work they did caused harm to indigenous people. In the twentieth century, Mennonite denominations in North America began banding together to do relief and development work through organizations such as Mennonite Central Committee, Mennonite Disaster Service, and Mennonite Economic Development Associates.

Especially in the last half of the twentieth century, Mennonites also began planting churches in North American cities, attracting people from a wide variety of ethnic backgrounds. Today there are thriving African American and Hispanic Mennonite churches, as well as other-language congregations comprised of immigrants. A small but significant group of Mennonites are in French-speaking Quebec. The stereotype that many North Americans have had of Mennonites—German-origin folks who dress plainly and keep to themselves—has been steadily breaking down.

By the 1920s a worldwide network of Mennonite churches was emerging; this network became known as the Mennonite World Conference. More and more, the new churches no longer saw themselves just as daughter churches of North America and

---

Voice A: For all of us here, this is our story as Anabaptists.

Voice B: But not all my ancestors came from Switzerland or Russia.

Voice A: That's not the point. Do you believe in believers baptism?

Voice B: Yes.

Voice A: Then you're an Anabaptist.

Voice B: Well now, there's more to it than that. You have to follow Jesus and everything.

Voice A: But the point is that the story isn't about an ethnic group; it is about anybody who wants to follow Jesus in the way Anabaptists do. I'm African American—I'm not blood-related to Conrad Grebel, but hey, I'm an Anabaptist Mennonite as much as anyone else. It's not something you're born into. It's something you choose.

Europe. They now became the ones who made disciples in their own communities and beyond. The church continued to grow in numbers, especially in India, Democratic Republic of Congo, Indonesia, and Ethiopia. At the year 2000, there were one million members worldwide in sixty countries; more than half were from countries outside of Europe and North America.

Although there is still plenty of room to become more faithful, it is awesome to think that in some small way the Mennonite Church is part of God's ancient promise to Abraham and Sarah: that through them "all the nations of the earth will be blessed." Who could have imagined what all God had in store?

I think one of the most wonderful things about us is that we are a *global* church. There are far more Anabaptists in the global south than in the United States and Canada.

Specific Anabaptist beliefs

Anabaptists today—including Mennonites—generally accept the core beliefs that other Christians have held for centuries. The Apostles' Creed is an ancient summary of those beliefs (see sidebar). But ever since the Schleitheim Confession (see p. 166), Anabaptists have stated their specific beliefs in various ways. One reference point today for members of Mennonite Church Canada and Mennonite Church USA, for example, is the *Confession of Faith in a Mennonite Perspective*, which is summarized on page 183. Here is a summary of specific Anabaptist beliefs:

Believers baptism is an important step of faith. Many Christian churches baptize babies who later "confirm" their faith publicly after a period of instruction. Anabaptists believe the Bible teaches that baptism should follow a person's decision to follow Jesus. Children cannot make that decision, and are safe in God's care until they can. When they can understand and make choices about their spiritual lives, children enter what we call the "age of

The Apostles' Creed (381 CE, Rome)

I believe in God, the Father almighty, creator of heaven and earth.

I believe in Jesus Christ, God's only Son, our Lord, who was conceived by the Holy Spirit, born of the Virgin Mary, suffered under Pontius Pilate, was crucified, died, and was buried; he descended to the dead. On the third day he rose again; he ascended into heaven, he is seated at the right hand of the Father, and he will come again to judge the living and the dead.

I believe in the Holy Spirit, the holy catholic church, the communion of saints, the forgiveness of sins, the resurrection of the body, and the life everlasting. Amen.[21]

accountability." Believers make a public commitment to follow Jesus, and that is evident in how they live their lives. That is why Anabaptists value the idea of a "visible church."

Jesus is the standard for our Christian living. Many Christians emphasize the importance of having the right set of belief or rituals. Anabaptists believe that following Jesus is at the heart of our faith. When in doubt about what is the right thing to do, we look at what Jesus did and taught as our standard (Hebrews 1:1–3). It's true that some of the things Jesus asks us to do seem impossible, like loving our enemies. But we believe that with the Spirit's help we are called to live the life he taught. Many Anabaptists have had no problem reciting the Apostles' Creed, but they would also want to emphasize the life and teachings of Jesus, not just his birth, death, and resurrection.

Our faith is both public and private. Some Christians believe that we can divide our lives in two—private and public. In their private lives, these believers follow Jesus. But in their public lives, their top responsibility goes to the government or to their job. For example, if the state asks them to fight in a war, they do it. If they accept Jesus' call to love enemies, that is reserved for the private side of life. Anabaptists believe that the same ethics apply Monday and Sunday, in public and private.

The church is a living community of God's new people. In some Christian traditions, the church is a place for individuals to hear inspiration from the Bible, worship, and receive the rites of the church from religious professionals. Anabaptists say that *all* members share in the church's work. We use our spiritual gifts to build up the church. We know that by ourselves we won't hear God perfectly, and we won't have the strength to live out our calling. That's

---

Voice A: Everyone says we're supposed to follow the Bible, but the Bible says different things on certain subjects. Take war, for example. Parts of the Bible make it seem like God condones war. But then you read statements by Isaiah or Jesus or Paul, and it seems God would say no to war. What are you supposed to do with that apparent conflict?

Michele: Christians have several different approaches to solve this problem. Some divide up their ethics depending on whether they're for groups or for individuals, and you only have to obey the teachings of Jesus for personal ethical issues. Others say we only have to obey his teachings after Jesus returns. Anabaptists say that when the Bible seems to have internal disagreements, you do what Jesus said and did. Why? Because Jesus is God in the flesh (Hebrews 1:1–3).

why we submit ourselves to one another for correction and support. In the church we care enough about each other to speak the truth in love, confessing our faults and forgiving each other. We don't just leave when things don't go our way. We know we need each other.

God calls us to work for peace and justice. Some Christians believe that in certain circumstances, God is in favor of using violence to achieve goals. Anabaptists disagree. If Jesus' life and teaching are our standard, and if we are truly empowered by the Spirit to live like Jesus did, then living nonviolently and working for the shalom of all people are the natural outcomes. That is why Mennonites not only oppose war, but also work to take away the conditions—such as poverty and oppression—that cause violence and war. We do not believe, as some Christians do, that God really cares only about spiritual salvation. We are called to feed the hungry, clothe the naked, and visit those in prison out of the heartfelt love that flows out of us . . . just like Jesus did.

The Bible is the guiding text to teach us about God's will. All of the points above rest on how we view the Bible. Most Christian denominations (including Anabaptists) affirm that the Bible is inspired by God (2 Timothy 3:16). The Scriptures can thus be trusted for our faith and life (Proverbs 30:5). More than many other denominations, however, Anabaptists emphasize that the Scriptures should be interpreted Christocentrically. That is, we believe that Jesus Christ is the clearest picture of God, and of what God's ultimate will is for us (John 1:14, 18; Hebrews 1:1–3). So, when the Bible seems to give us different messages about a certain topic (like war), we look at what Jesus says first and interpret everything else in scripture in light of Jesus.

Tips on using the Bible to guide your decision-making

1. Don't cut and paste, taking verses out of their context. Read each Bible passage in light of the whole story.
2. Use the story of Jesus as the measuring stick in figuring out what the Bible says. When in doubt, ask, "What would Jesus do?"
3. Obey what is already clear. An elderly Mennonite pastor once said, "If you don't understand Scripture, obey what is already clearly spelled out—like feeding the poor, loving all people. Doing this will help you figure out the rest." (See also John 7:17.)
4. Find out about the culture and history of the time when the Bible passage was written.
5. Ask others. Studying the Bible in community helps us all learn together.
6. Pray. Jesus promised that the Holy Spirit would guide us into truth (John 16:13).

Michele: What do you think the church will look like in ten years?

Voice A: Church will be seen as something bigger than what we do on Sunday morning.

Voice B: We'll care more about climate change and solving poverty and racism.

Voice C: We won't care about all the rules so much.

Voice D: But hopefully, we will be so overwhelmed with the love of Jesus that we will just draw all sorts of people and they won't be turned away by our high standards.

Voice C: High standards? Maybe just the one standard that everyone can do? That is, following Jesus.

Voice B: High standards that won't be mandatory?

Voice C: Yeah, I mean, it's the grace and holiness thing again.

What the future will hold

While it's anyone's guess as to what the church will look like ten years from now, the Bible gives us some idea of what will happen to the church and the world at the end of time. Jesus promised that he would come again in victory over death. Paul and the other New Testament writers clearly show the early church's conviction that Jesus will come again and that believers should be ready. And when Christ comes again, God will make all things right in the world. That will be the grand finale to God's story and our story.

Here are a few key points from the Bible:

- *The reign of God has already begun.* When Jesus started his work, his main message was "The kingdom of God has come near; repent, and believe in the good news" (Mark 1:15). In his teaching he emphasized that the reign of God is here among us (Luke 17:20–21). One of the paradoxes of Christianity is that while the reign of God will come to full realization at the end of the ages (see below), it is already here. As George Ladd put it, God's rule is "already" but "not yet" at the same time.[22]

- *Jesus will return to earth.* Jesus spoke of his return often (Matthew 24–25; Mark 13; John 1–7), and the angel confirmed it when Jesus returned to heaven (Acts 1:11). When he comes, it will not be like his first coming as a small baby, when only a few recognized him as the Messiah. Jesus will come in might and honor (Matthew 24:30; Acts 1:11; see also Daniel 7:9–14).
- *Jesus' victory will be of truth and justice, not military might.* The book of Revelation depicts a final war against evil and against Satan (Revelation 19:11–16). Like many other things in Revelation, however, this war is symbolic and spiritual. Jesus appears as the "Word of God," and the only weapon he has is a sharp sword coming out of his mouth—a symbol of the word of God (Ephesians 6:17; Hebrews 4:12). The God who created the world with a mighty word will come again and bring back order and justice with the same tool—the Word. The righteous will be blessed with eternal life, and the wicked will be judged (John 5:28–29; Revelation 21:1–8).
- *Evil will be defeated the only way it can be—through nonviolent obedience to God.* The book of Revelation speaks of a dragon, symbolizing evil. "But they [Christians] have conquered him [the dragon] by the blood of the Lamb and by the word of their testimony, for they did not cling to life even in the face of death" (Revelation 12:11). This gives us a powerful picture of how the death and resurrection of Jesus are still at the center of God's defeat of evil, and how Jesus' followers also join in the victory through giving up their own lives.

Jesus, often depicted in Revelation as the nonviolent Lamb who was killed, was the model and the encouragement for the persecuted Christians of the first century. Today, too, when

---

Then I saw a new heaven and a new earth, for the first heaven and the first earth had passed away, and the sea was no more. And I saw the holy city, the new Jerusalem, coming down out of heaven from God. . . . And I heard a loud voice from the throne saying, "See, the home of God is among mortals. He will dwell with them; they will be his peoples, and God himself will be with them and be their God; he will wipe every tear from their eyes. Death will be no more; mourning and crying and pain will be no more, for the first things have passed away." And the one who was seated on the throne said, "See, I am making all things new."

—Revelation 21:1–2a, 3–5a

A strange and wonderful book

The book of Revelation is more than just a message about how the story will end. It also gives us a series of mysterious pictures of how God's kingdom is victorious over the evil of this world, even though it doesn't look like it to us. To name only a few, we see a throne in heaven surrounded by white-robed people and strange creatures worshiping God (Revelation 4); beasts and dragons defeated by a Lamb (12–14); a dazzling, cube-shaped city, being lowered from heaven (21). It is more like an abstract painting than a photograph.

While Christians throughout history have tried to use Revelation as a roadmap for end-times events, Revelation's words, like wild paint strokes, are there to help us feel emotion more than present exact literal details about what will happen. We must remember that this strange conclusion to the Bible was really written as an encouragement for persecuted Christians between 90 and 100 CE. These believers needed some reassurance that God would see them through at a time when evil governments seemed to be all-powerful.

The main message of Revelation was for them, and is for us, to follow Jesus and stand firm in our faith, and everything will work out.

times get scary and we wonder what we are supposed to do in the face of awful evil, we "follow the Lamb wherever he goes" (Revelation 14:4). We live as Jesus lived, in nonviolent love and through the power of the Spirit.

- *The church is called to live out the justice and peace of the reign of God right now, anticipating the love and peace of the age to come.* We know things aren't perfect and that sin has a lot of power in this world. But through the power of Jesus, the people of God can start living out kingdom values now (Matthew 5–7). The church is not the same thing as the kingdom of God, nor can we bring the kingdom of God into its fulfillment by our own strength. But we are witnesses to the kingdom and proof that through Jesus we can do hard things such as sharing our wealth and loving our enemies.
- *Believers are to be ready for Jesus' return.* Jesus may come earlier (Matthew 24:45–51) or later than we expect (25:1–13).

Jesus tells us clearly that we can't know the hour or day. And we don't have to worry about not knowing this day, because we know what to do to get ready. We serve and follow Jesus in faithful obedience, using our God-given talents (25:14–30) and caring for those in need (25:31–46).

The main point of what the Bible says about the end of time is that God ultimately defeats the powers of sin and death. Following Peter's confession of Jesus as the Christ, Jesus said, "On this rock I will build my church, and the gates of Hades will not prevail against it" (16:18). God will not abandon the church, neither the Mennonite church nor the larger church. God will work through all of us to build the reign of God as we follow Jesus, even if it means sacrifice and suffering. As we follow, we can have joy in knowing we are doing the right thing, the joy of having meaning in our lives, and the joy of being in relationship with the One who loves us best.

Voice A: I just wish I could see more miracles. Or not even so much miracles, but just see God at work right now. You say the Story is ongoing, but it's hard to see that in our day-to-day living.

And it's hard to believe that God would use someone ordinary like me to keep the Story going.

Michele: Jesus says that even a cup of cold water that is given in his name makes a difference (Mark 9:41). And if we saw miracles all the time, would we start to follow Jesus just for the spiritual high? I think we have to choose to have faith, even when we don't feel it, but we also have the faith to keep asking for miracles. I think we have to choose to believe that Jesus is working through us, in miraculous ways, and we have to choose this especially on the ordinary days. We may never know what our cup of cold water has done for others on this side of heaven, but that's okay, because we are loved. Jesus loves us more than we'll ever know. And the more we live with him, the more we feel his love and feel compelled to share it with others. Maybe that's really the miracle we need.

The Story continues

Whether Jesus comes tomorrow or in a thousand years, we live today in the midst of God's Story. Isn't that amazing? The story of Abraham and Sarah, of the twelve disciples, of Mary and Martha, of Paul, Lydia, Timothy, and countless other faithful Christians throughout history—this is our story, too, if we choose it.

If we choose this story as our story, everything changes. We choose to believe that there is more to this world than the things we can see and touch. We choose to believe that true joy comes not from money or fame, but from saying yes to God's plan for our lives. We choose to see a different reality shaped by God's

Story. We choose Jesus, just as God, long before we were born, chose us.

As we say yes to Jesus and commit ourselves to a dynamic relationship with him, the power of sin is broken. Our relationships are restored. We have a new identity. We are free. We are changed. And we respond in love and gratitude. Our spiritual disciplines and our service to others flow naturally out of who we now are. We find meaning and purpose and joy not out of what we do or how much money we make, but out of who we are in Christ.

This journey is ongoing, full of ups and downs, and maybe raises more questions than we have answers for. But we do not travel alone. We have all of our siblings in Christ, and we have the Holy Spirit as close to us as our own breath. We love and serve a God who is all-powerful, yet who came to us as a baby in humility, a God who is both holy and merciful. We walk and talk with the very Creator of the universe. This journey, this salvation, is completely free and yet costs us everything. It's hard, yet it's also the most wonderful journey there is.

But we have to choose it. Every one of us is confronted with two basic stories in life. Dominant culture says, "Live for yourself!" Jesus says, "If any wish to come after me, let them deny themselves and take up their cross daily and follow me. For those who want to save their life will lose it, and those who lose their life for my sake will save it. For what does it profit them if they gain the whole world but lose or forfeit themselves?" (Luke 9:23–25).

You *will* be part of some story, you *will* take some journey, but whose will it be? How you decide that question affects everything in your life. The Story waits to become your story. What do you say? What will you do?

A spiritual discipline to practice

Draw a timeline of your life. Create some symbols and write a legend for what the symbols mean. For example, if your timeline goes down, it symbolizes a more difficult time in your life; stars mean major turning points; jagged lines mean stress, etc. Try to include every major event in your life up to date. This is your story in a drawing. Now take time in silence and just listen to what God has to say to you. Then speak to God about each event, both thanking God and asking for a renewed sense of peace and God's presence in your life.

APPENDIXES

A Note about the Body of Christ

MANY PEOPLE AMONG US are LGBTQ, which represents a wide spectrum of particular sexual orientations and gender identities. What's new is that now more than in earlier times, we are acknowledging their presence, and we're grappling with theology and feelings. Our LGBTQ friends have had feelings about this for a long time—centuries. But earlier catechisms have not included discussions about this issue and this catechism will.

It's important to distinguish between gender identity and particular ethical behaviors. This book will only work to address the following question: Who is a member of God's family and on what basis? The New Testament answer to that question is that all persons who follow the way of Jesus are members of God's family. This book will assume the validity of the science that says that persons don't choose their sexual orientation or gender identity. It also assumes the truth that all humans are made in the image of God.

I grew up embracing a traditional understanding that the Bible only supported a heterosexual marriage. I used to think that people had a choice about their sexual orientation. But I've changed my mind. I've heard story after story from young adults who tried to "pray the gay away" for a decade, stories of people who love Jesus with all their hearts and they know they are queer, people who exemplify the fruits of the Spirit daily. Like the religious leaders in John 9, I was faced with some cognitive dissonance. Jesus healed a man blind from birth. Jesus expressly said this man did not sin to cause his condition, and Jesus not only healed him but did so on the Sabbath. And like the religious leaders who were skeptical in the face of unexpected evidence, I've seen people who have the Spirit of God living in them, people who are whole, just as they are. I needed to decide if I could "see" with new eyes.

I have decided to see with new eyes.

At least on some level, I think I understand readers of this book who might be on the other side and hold the more traditional view that says Christians can't affirm persons who are LGBTQ. I believe that you, too, are in deep anguish over this issue, because you love people who are LGBTQ, you love the Bible, and you just want to do the right thing. I hear you.

This theological question is particularly dicey because we are afraid that if we affirm our queer friends, then we are going against scripture, and once you start down that path, where is the end? Does this lead to affirming just about anything we want to affirm? Again, I hear this concern, and sometimes wake up to this fear myself in the middle of the night.

But I have two responses to this fear. First, the writer of 1 John 4:18 says, "Perfect love casts out fear." I take this to mean that we can't let fear keep us from doing what we believe is the right thing to do, which, in this case, is to affirm those persons who have a different gender identity or sexual orientation. We can't let fear dictate our sense of right and wrong. Second, I can't let my fear of being too inclusive keep me from listening to the Living Word. As Anabaptist Mennonite Christians, we believe that Jesus is the Word of God, and not the Bible. We believe that the Bible itself says this (see Hebrews 1:1–3 and the story in Acts 10). And while this assertion may appear scary, because interpreting life through the lens of Jesus seems like more of a moving target than words written on a page, we still want to be biblical believers. We want to do the right thing.

Perhaps the right thing to do is to look in the eyes of someone who is proclaiming Jesus as Lord and living out the fruits of the Spirit and say, "Yes, you are God's beloved, exactly the way you are."

It is my hope that we remember that we are one community, one body of Christ. That we are better together, closer to the heart of God when we live and work together and hear each other's stories and acknowledge each other's pain. I know that Mennonite Church USA and Mennonite Church Canada have been on different timetables concerning this issue. Not everyone is at the same place. But we have common understandings about Jesus, about justice and peace, and about many other things. We have committed ourselves to loving and serving each other, and this book seeks to strengthen those bonds, even while it asks some questions that are uncomfortable.

Please, let's keep talking. Let's stay together.

A Confession of Faith Summary

1. We believe that **God** exists and is pleased with all who draw near by faith. We worship the one holy and loving God who is Father, Son, and Holy Spirit eternally. God has created all things visible and invisible, has brought salvation and new life to humanity through Jesus Christ, and continues to sustain the church and all things until the end of the age.

2. We believe in **Jesus Christ**, the Word of God become flesh. He is the Savior of the world, who has delivered us from the dominion of sin and reconciled us to God by his death on a cross. He was declared to be Son of God by his resurrection from the dead. He is the head of the church, the exalted Lord, the Lamb who was slain, coming again to reign with God in glory.

3. We believe in the **Holy Spirit**, the eternal Spirit of God, who dwelled in Jesus Christ, who empowers the church, who is the source of our life in Christ, and who is poured out on those who believe as the guarantee of redemption.

4. We believe that all **Scripture** is inspired by God through the Holy Spirit for instruction in salvation and training in righteousness. We accept the Scriptures as the Word of God and as the fully reliable and trustworthy standard for Christian faith and life. Led by the Holy Spirit in the church, we interpret Scripture in harmony with Jesus Christ.

5. We believe that God has **created the heavens and the earth** and all that is in them, and that God preserves and renews what has been made. All creation has its source outside itself and belongs to the Creator. The world has been created good because God is good and provides all that is needed for life.

6. We believe that God has **created human beings** in the divine image. God formed them from the dust of the earth and gave them a special dignity among all the works of creation. Human beings have been made for relationship with God, to live in peace with each other, and to take care of the rest of creation.

7. We confess that, beginning with Adam and Eve, humanity has disobeyed God, given way to the tempter, and chosen to **sin**. All have fallen short of the Creator's intent, marred the image of God in which they were created, disrupted order in the world, and limited their love for others. Because of sin, humanity has been given over to the enslaving powers of evil and death.

8. We believe that, through Jesus Christ, God offers **salvation** from sin and a new way of life. We receive God's salvation when we repent and accept Jesus Christ as Savior and Lord. In Christ, we are reconciled with God and brought into the reconciling community. We place our faith in God that, by the same power that raised Christ from the dead, we may be saved from sin to follow Christ and to know the fullness of salvation.

9. We believe that the **church** is the assembly of those who have accepted God's offer of salvation through faith in Jesus Christ. It is the new community of disciples sent into the world to proclaim the reign of God and to provide a foretaste of the church's glorious hope. It is the new society established and sustained by the Holy Spirit.

10. We believe that the **mission** of the church is to proclaim and to be a sign of the kingdom of God. Christ has commissioned the church to make disciples of all nations, baptizing them, and teaching them to observe all things he has commanded.

11. We believe that the **baptism** of believers with water is a sign of their cleansing from sin. Baptism is also a pledge before the church of their covenant with God to walk in the way of Jesus Christ through the power of the Holy Spirit. Believers are baptized into Christ and his body by the Spirit, water, and blood.

12. We believe that the **Lord's Supper** is a sign by which the church thankfully remembers the new covenant which Jesus established by his death. In this communion meal, the church renews its covenant with God and with each other and participates in the life and death of Jesus Christ, until he comes.

13. We believe that in **washing** the **feet** of his disciples, Jesus calls us to serve one another in love as he did. Thus we acknowledge our frequent need of cleansing, renew our willingness to let go of pride and worldly power, and offer our lives in humble service and sacrificial love.

14. We practice **discipline** in the church as a sign of God's offer of transforming grace. Discipline is intended to liberate erring brothers and sisters from sin, and to restore them to a right relationship with God and to fellowship in the church. The practice of discipline gives integrity to the church's witness in the world.

15. We believe that **ministry** is a continuation of the work of Christ, who gives gifts through the Holy Spirit to all believers and empowers them for service in the church and in the world. We also believe that God calls particular persons in the church to specific leadership ministries and offices. All who minister are accountable to God and to the community of faith.

16. We believe that the church of Jesus Christ is **one body** with many members, ordered in such a way that, through the one Spirit, believers may be built together spiritually into a dwelling place for God.

17. We believe that Jesus Christ calls us to **discipleship**, to take up our cross and follow him. Through the gift of God's saving grace, we are empowered to be disciples of Jesus, filled with his Spirit, following his teachings and his path through suffering to new life. As we are faithful to his way, we become conformed to Christ and separated from the evil in the world.

18. We believe that to be a disciple of Jesus is to know **life in the Spirit**. As the life, death, and resurrection of Jesus Christ takes shape in us, we grow in the image of Christ and in our relationship with God. The Holy Spirit is active in individual and in communal worship, leading us deeper into the experience of God.

19. We believe that God intends human life to begin in **families** and to be blessed through families. Even more, God desires all people to become part of the church, God's family. As single and married members of the church family give and receive nurture and healing, families can grow toward the wholeness that God intends. We are called to chastity and to loving faithfulness in marriage.

20. We commit ourselves to tell the **truth**, to give a simple yes or no, and to avoid the swearing of oaths.

21. We believe that everything belongs to God, who calls the church to live in faithful **stewardship** of all that God has entrusted to us, and to participate now in the rest and justice which God has promised.

22. We believe that **peace** is the will of God. God created the world in peace, and God's peace is most fully revealed in Jesus Christ, who is our peace and the peace of the whole world. Led by the Holy Spirit, we follow Christ in the way of peace, doing justice, bringing reconciliation, and practicing nonresistance, even in the face of violence and warfare.

23. We believe that the church is God's holy nation, called to give full allegiance to Christ its head and to witness to every **nation, government, and society** about God's saving love.

24. We place our hope in the **reign of God** and its fulfillment in the day when Christ will come again in glory to judge the living and the dead. He will gather his church, which is already living under the reign of God. We await God's final victory, the end of this present age of struggle, the resurrection of the dead, and a new heaven and a new earth. There the people of God will reign with Christ in justice, righteousness, and peace for ever and ever.

Acknowledgments

Finding Ourselves in God's Story has been a journey of love. I've spent countless hours with youth and young adults, talking about faith and life, talking about what really matters. And I've spent more hours talking with other theologians and editors, trying to get just the right word, just the right nuance. It's a journey few have taken in quite this way, and it has all been about love.

The conversations themselves were key. In all of life, caring conversations are an essential part of finding ourselves in God's Story. None of us alone can know God in entirety. We need each other to help us see parts of God's heart that are otherwise hidden to us. The conversations also nurture loving relationships, and that's what God desires. That's the main point of the Bible, God's story. Knowing God goes deeper than knowing about God, than knowing all the right doctrines. There is a truth more complex than all our wisdom. We find God in relationship, which always has some ambiguity and mess. As I wrote this book, I practiced loving other people who disagree with me, changing my mind sometimes but not capitulating all my cherished beliefs. This was the most difficult part of the journey, but also the most rewarding.

I want to thank all the youth and young adults who joined me in conversations, whether they were in Kansas City at the

Mennonite convention, or in other places around kitchen tables. You all are my hope, my assurance that the church will not only survive but thrive. I also want to thank my editors, David Cramer, Elisabeth Ivey, and Rachel Elaine Martens, for their work on behalf of this book. I'm especially grateful for Amy Gingerich, who gave me wisdom and support. Finally, I want to thank my husband Del Hershberger for his love and encouragement when the journey was difficult.

Notes

1 Raj Persaud, "Is Becoming Famous Hazardous to Your Health?," *Psychology Today*, November 2, 2023, https://www.psychologytoday.com/ us/blog/ slightly-blighty/202310/the-potentially-fatal-downsides-of-being -famous.

2 Paul D. Miller, "What Is Christian Nationalism?," *Christianity Today*, February 2, 2021, https://www.christianitytoday.com/2021/02/what-is -christian-nationalism/.

3 Christian Smith with Melinda Lundquist Denton, *Soul Searching: The Religious and Spiritual Lives of American Teenagers* (Oxford: Oxford University Press, 2005), 162–70.

4 Chap Clark, *Hurt: Inside the World of Today's Teenagers* (Grand Rapids: Baker Academic, 2004), 23–56.

5 Perry Yoder, *Shalom: The Bible's Word for Salvation, Justice and Peace* (Eugene: Wipf and Stock, 2017), 10–19.

6 Marcus J. Borg and N. T. Wright, *The Meaning of Jesus: Two Visions* (New York: Harper Collins, 1999), 171–78.

7 Don Blosser with Timothy J. Dailey, Randy Petersen, and Dietrich Gruen, *Jesus: His Life and Times* (Lincolnwood: Publications International, 1999), 86.

8 Marjorie J. Thompson, *Soul Feast: An Invitation to the Christian Spiritual Life* (Louisville: Westminster John Knox, 1995), 8–9.

9 Richard J. Foster, *Celebration of Discipline: The Path to Spiritual Growth* (New York: Harper Collins, 1998), 1–11.

10 Mark Yaconelli, "Focusing Youth Ministry through Christian Practices," in *Starting Right: Thinking Theologically about Youth Ministry*, ed. Kenda Creasy Dean, Chap Clark, and Dave Rahn (Grand Rapids: Zondervan, 2001), 156.

11 Walter Klaassen, *Anabaptism in Outline* (Scottdale: Herald Press, 1981), 87, quoted in C. Arnold Snyder, *Anabaptist History and Theology: An Introduction* (Kitchener: Pandora Press, 1995), 164.

12 English translation of the Lord's Prayer, © 1998, English Language Liturgical Consultation (ELLC), and used by permission, www.englishtexts.org.

13 Foster, *Celebration of Discipline*, 2.

14 David Augsburger, *Helping People Forgive* (Louisville: Westminster John Knox, 1996), 68–72.

15 Foster, *Celebration of Discipline*, 2.

16 Perry Thomas, *Exploring Church History: 20 Centuries of Christ's People* (Nashville: World, 2005), 6–7.

17 Tertullian, *Apologeticus*, 197 CE. *The Apology of Tertullian for the Christians, Translated with Introduction, Analysis, and Appendix Containing the Letters of Pliny and Trajan Respecting the Christians by T. H. Bindley* (London & Oxford: Parker & Co., 1890), xvi, 158.

18 "The Christians in the World," from a letter to Diognetus, https://www.vatican.va/spirit/documents/spirit_20010522_diogneto_en.html.

19 Menno Simons, *The Complete Writings of Menno Simons, c. 1496–1561*, trans. Leonard Verduin, ed. J. C. Wenger (Scottdale: Herald Press), 1956.

20 Troy Osborne, *Radicals and Reformers: A Survey of Global Anabaptist History* (Harrisonburg: Herald Press, 2024), 82–92 and 216–19.

21 Apostles' Creed, https://www.usccb.org/prayers/apostles-creed.

22 George Eldon Ladd, *The Gospel of the Kingdom: Scriptural Studies in the Kingdom of God* (Grand Rapids: Eerdmans, 1959), 27.

The Author

Michele Hershberger is the author of *God's Story, Our Story*; *A Christian View of Hospitality*; and several other books. She serves as Bible faculty and co–campus pastor at Hesston College (KS), where she teaches Bible and youth ministry classes. With a degree from Associated Mennonite Biblical Seminary, Hershberger has devoted her life to serving the church as a pastor, writer, speaker, and instructor. She and her husband Del Hershberger have three children and are members of Hesston Mennonite Church.